The Gondoliers by Gilbert & Sullivan

or The King of Barataria

Libretto by William S. Gilbert
Music by Arthur Sullivan

The partnership between William Schwenck Gilbert and Arthur Seymour Sullivan and their canon of Savoy Operas is rightly lauded by all lovers of comic opera the world over.

Gilbert's sharp, funny words and Sullivan's deliciously lively and hummable tunes create a world that is distinctly British in view but has the world as its audience.

Both men were exceptionally talented and gifted in their own right and wrote much, often with other partners, that still stands the test of time. However, together as a team they created Light or Comic Operas of a standard that have had no rivals equal to their standard, before or since. That's quite an achievement.

To be recognised by the critics is one thing but their commercial success was incredible. The profits were astronomical, allowing for the building of their own purpose built theatre – The Savoy Theatre.

Beginning with the first of their fourteen collaborations, Thespis in 1871 and travelling through many classics including The Sorcerer (1877), H.M.S. Pinafore (1878), The Pirates of Penzance (1879), The Mikado (1885), The Gondoliers (1889) to their finale in 1896 with The Grand Duke, Gilbert & Sullivan created a legacy that is constantly revived and admired in theatres and other media to this very day.

Index of Contents

The Gondoliers, or, The King of Barataria, was the twelfth opera written by Gilbert and Sullivan. It opened on December 7, 1889 at the Savoy Theatre, and ran for 554 performances

DRAMATIS PERSONAE
THE DUKE OF PLAZA-TORO (a Grandee of Spain)
LUIZ (his attendant)

DON ALHAMBRA DEL BOLERO (the Grand Inquisitioner)

Venetian Gondoliers
MARCO PALMIERI
GIUSEPPE PALMIERI
ANTONIO
FRANCESCO
GIORGIO
ANNIBALE

THE DUCHESS OF PLAZA-TORO
CASILDA (her Daughter)

Contadine
GIANETTA
TESSA
FIAMETTA
VITTORIA
GIULIA

INEZ (the King's Foster-mother)

Chorus of Gondoliers and Contadine, Men-at-Arms, Heralds and Pages

SCENES
ACT I - The Piazzetta, Venice
ACT II - Pavilion in the Palace of Barataria

(An interval of three months is supposed to elapse between Acts I and II)

DATE - 1750

MUSICAL NUMBERS
Overture
ACT I
1. List and learn (Gondoliers, Antonio, Marco, Giuseppe, and Chorus of Contadine)
2. From the sunny Spanish shore (Duke, Duchess, Casilda, and Luiz)
3. In enterprise of martial kind (Duke with Duchess, Casilda, and Luiz)
4. O rapture, when alone together (Casilda and Luiz)
5. There was a time (Casilda and Luiz)
6. I stole the prince (Don Alhambra with Duke, Duchess, Casilda, and Luiz)
7. But, bless my heart (Casilda and Don Alhambra)
8. Try we life-long (Duke, Duchess, Casilda, Luiz, and Don Alhambra)
9. Bridegroom and bride (Chorus)

ACT I

Scene.— the Piazzetta, Venice. The Ducal Palace on the right.

FIAMETTA, GIULIA, VITTORIA, and other CONTADINE discovered, each tying a bouquet of roses.

CHORUS OF CONTADINE
List and learn, ye dainty roses,
Roses white and roses red,
Why we bind you into posies
Ere your morning bloom has fled.
By a law of maiden's making,
Accents of a heart that's aching,
Even though that heart be breaking,
Should by maiden be unsaid:
Though they love with love exceeding,
They must seem to be unheeding—
Go ye then and do their pleading,
Roses white and roses red!

FIAMETTA
Two there are for whom in duty,
Every maid in Venice sighs—
Two so peerless in their beauty
That they shame the summer skies.
We have hearts for them, in plenty,
They have hearts, but all too few,
We, alas, are four-and-twenty!
They, alas, are only two!

We, alas!

CHORUS
Alas!

FIAMETTA
Are four-and-twenty,
They, alas!

CHORUS
Alas!

FIAMETTA
Are only two.

CHORUS
They, alas, are only two, alas!
Now ye know, ye dainty roses,
Roses white and roses red,
Why we bind you into posies,
Ere your morning bloom has fled,
Roses white and roses red!

(During this chorus ANTONIO, FRANCESCO, GIORGIO, and other Gondoliers have entered unobserved by the Girls—at first two, then two more, then four, then half a dozen, then the remainder of the CHORUS.)

SOLI.

FRANCESCO
Good morrow, pretty maids; for whom prepare ye
These floral tributes extraordinary?

FIAMETTA
For Marco and Giuseppe Palmieri,
The pink and flower of all the Gondolieri.

GIULIA
They're coming here, as we have heard but lately,
To choose two brides from us who sit sedately.

ANTONIO
Do all you maidens love them?

ALL
Passionately!

ANTONIO
These gondoliers are to be envied greatly!

GIORGIO
But what of us, who one and all adore you?
Have pity on our passion, we implore you!

FIAMETTA
These gentlemen must make their choice before you;

VITTORIA
In the meantime we tacitly ignore you.

GIULIA
When they have chosen two that leaves you plenty—
Two dozen we, and ye are four-and-twenty.

FIAMETTA and VITTORIA
Till then, enjoy your dolce far niente.

ANTONIO
With pleasure, nobody contradicente!

SONG—**ANTONIO and CHORUS.**
For the merriest fellows are we, tra la,
That ply on the emerald sea, tra la;
With loving and laughing,
And quipping and quaffing,
We're happy as happy can be, tra la—
With loving and laughing, etc.

With sorrow we've nothing to do, tra la,
And care is a thing to pooh-pooh, tra la;
And Jealousy yellow,
Unfortunate fellow,
We drown in the shimmering blue, tra la—
And Jealousy yellow, etc.

FIAMETTA (looking off)
See, see, at last they come to make their choice—
Let us acclaim them with united voice.

(MARCO and GIUSEPPE appear in gondola at back.)

CHORUS (Girls)
Hail, hail! gallant gondolieri, ben venuti!
Accept our love, our homage, and our duty.
Ben' venuti! ben' venuti!

(MARCO and GIUSEPPE jump ashore—the GIRLS salute them.)

DUET—**MARCO and GIUSEPPE, with CHORUS OF GIRLS.**

MARCO and GIULIA
Buon' giorno, signorine!

GIRLS
Gondolieri carissimi!
Siamo contadine!

MARCO and GIULIA (bowing)
Servitori umilissimi!
Per chi questi fiori—
Questi fiori bellissimi?

GIRLS
Per voi, bei signori
O eccellentissimi!

(The GIRLS present their bouquets to MARCO and GIUSEPPE, who are overwhelmed with them, and carry them with difficulty.)

MARCO and GIUSEPPE (their arms full of flowers)
O ciel'! O ciel'!

GIRLS
Buon' giorno, cavalieri!

MARCO and GIUSEPPE (deprecatingly)
Siamo gondolieri.

(To FIAMETTA and VITTORIA)
Signorina, io t' amo!

GIRLS (deprecatingly)
Contadine siamo.

MARCO and GIUSEPPE
Signorine!

GIRLS (deprecatingly)
Contadine!

(Curtseying to MARCO and GIUSEPPE)

Cavalieri.

MARCO and GIUSEPPE (deprecatingly)

Gondolieri!
Poveri gondolieri!

CHORUS
Buon' giorno, signorine, etc.

DUET—**MARCO and GIUSEPPE**
We're called gondolieri,
But that's a vagary,
It's quite honorary
The trade that we ply.
For gallantry noted
Since we were short-coated,
To beauty devoted,
Giuseppe\Are Marco and I;

When morning is breaking,
Our couches forsaking,
To greet their awaking
With carols we come.
At summer day's nooning,
When weary lagooning,
Our mandolins tuning,
We lazily thrum.

When vespers are ringing,
To hope ever clinging,
With songs of our singing
A vigil we keep,
When daylight is fading,
Enwrapt in night's shading,
With soft serenading
We sing them to sleep.

We're called gondolieri, etc.

RECITATIVE—**MARCO and GIUSEPPE**

MARCO
And now to choose our brides!

GIUSEPPE
As all are young and fair,
And amiable besides,

BOTH
We really do not care
A preference to declare.

MARCO
A bias to disclose
Would be indelicate—

GIUSEPPE
And therefore we propose
To let impartial Fate
Select for us a mate!

ALL
Viva!

GIRLS
A bias to disclose
Would be indelicate—

MEN
But how do they propose
To let impartial Fate
Select for them a mate?

GIUSEPPE
These handkerchiefs upon our eyes be good enough to bind,

MARCO
And take good care that both of us are absolutely blind;

BOTH
Then turn us round—and we, with all convenient despatch,
Will undertake to marry any two of you we catch!

ALL
Viva!
They undertake to marry any two of us\them they catch!

(The GIRLS prepare to bind their eyes as directed.)

FIAMETTA (to MARCO)
Are you peeping?
Can you see me?

MARCO
Dark I'm keeping,
Dark and dreamy!

(MARCO slyly lifts bandage.)

VITTORIA (to GIUSEPPE)
If you're blinded
Truly, say so

GIUSEPPE
All right-minded
Players play so!

(Slyly lifts bandage).

FIAMETTA (detecting MARCO)
Conduct shady!
They are cheating!
Surely they de-
Serve a beating!

(Replaces bandage).

VITTORIA (detecting GIUSEPPE)
This too much is;
Maidens mocking—
Conduct such is
Truly shocking!

(Replaces bandage).

ALL
You can spy, sir!
Shut your eye, sir!
You may use it by and by, sir!
You can see, sir!
Don't tell me, sir!
That will do—now let it be, sir!

CHORUS OF GIRLS
My papa he keeps three horses,
Black, and white, and dapple grey, sir;
Turn three times, then take your courses,
Catch whichever girl you may, sir!

CHORUS OF MEN
My papa, etc.

(MARCO and GIUSEPPE turn round, as directed, and try to catch the girls. Business of blind-man's buff. Eventually MARCO catches GIANETTA, and GIUSEPPE catches TESSA. The two girls try to escape, but in vain. The two men pass their hands over the girls' faces to discover their identity.)

GIUSEPPE

I've at length achieved a capture!
(Guessing.) This is Tessa! (removes bandage). Rapture, rapture!

CHORUS
Rapture, rapture!

MARCO (guessing)
To me Gianetta fate has granted!

(Removes bandage).

Just the very girl I wanted!

CHORUS
Just the very girl he wanted!

GIUSEPPE (politely to MARCO)
If you'd rather change—

TESSA
My goodness!
This indeed is simple rudeness.

MARCO (politely to GIUSEPPE)
I've no preference whatever—

GIANETTA
Listen to him! Well, I never!

(Each man kisses each girl.)

GIANETTA
Thank you, gallant gondolieri!
In a set and formal measure
It is scarcely necessary
To express our pleasure.
Each of us to prove a treasure,
Conjugal and monetary,
Gladly will devote our leisure,
Gay and gallant gondolieri.
Tra, la, la, la, la, la, etc.

TESSA
Gay and gallant gondolieri,
Take us both and hold us tightly,
You have luck extraordinary;
We might both have been unsightly!
If we judge your conduct rightly,

'Twas a choice involuntary;
Still we thank you most politely,
Gay and gallant gondolieri!
Tra, la, la, la, la, la, etc.

CHORUS OF GIRLS
Thank you, gallant gondolieri;
In a set and formal measure,
It is scarcely necessary
To express our pleasure.
Each of us to prove a treasure
Gladly will devote our leisure,
Gay and gallant gondolieri!
Tra, la, la, la, la, la, etc.

ALL
Fate in this has put his finger—
Let us bow to Fate's decree,
Then no longer let us linger,
To the altar hurry we!

(They all dance off two and two—GIANETTA with MARCO, TESSA with GIUSEPPE.)

(Flourish. A gondola arrives at the Piazzetta steps, from which enter the DUKE of Plaza-toro, the DUCHESS, their daughter CASILDA, and their attendant LUIZ, who carries a drum. All are dressed in pompous but old and faded clothes.)

(Entrance of DUKE, DUCHESS, CASILDA, and LUIZ.)

DUKE
From the sunny Spanish shore,
The Duke of Plaza-Tor!—

DUCHESS
And His Grace's Duchess true—

CASILDA
And His Grace's daughter, too—

LUIZ
And His Grace's private drum
To Venetia's shores have come:

ALL
If ever, ever, ever
They get back to Spain,
They will never, never, never
Cross the sea again—

DUKE
Neither that Grandee from the Spanish shore,
The noble Duke of Plaza-Tor'—

DUCHESS
Nor His Grace's Duchess, staunch and true—

CASILDA
You may add, His Grace's daughter, too—

LUIZ
Nor His Grace's own particular drum
To Venetia's shores will come:

ALL
If ever, ever, ever
They get back to Spain,
They will never, never, never
Cross the sea again!

DUKE
At last we have arrived at our destination. This is the Ducal Palace, and it is here that the Grand Inquisitor resides. As a Castilian hidalgo of ninety-five quarterings, I regret that I am unable to pay my state visit on a horse. As a Castilian hidalgo of that description, I should have preferred to ride through the streets of Venice; but owing, I presume, to an unusually wet season, the streets are in such a condition that equestrian exercise is impracticable. No matter. Where is our suite?

LUIZ (coming forward)
Your Grace, I am here.

DUCHESS
 Why do you not do yourself the honour to kneel when you address His Grace?

DUKE
My love, it is so small a matter! (To LUIZ.) Still, you may as well do it.

(LUIZ kneels.)

CASILDA
The young man seems to entertain but an imperfect appreciation of the respect due from a menial to a Castilian hidalgo.

DUKE
My child, you are hard upon our suite.

CASILDA

Papa, I've no patience with the presumption of persons in his plebeian position. If he does not appreciate that position, let him be whipped until he does.

DUKE
Let us hope the omission was not intended as a slight. I should be much hurt if I thought it was. So would he. (To LUIZ.) Where are the halberdiers who were to have had the honour of meeting us here, that our visit to the Grand Inquisitor might be made in becoming state?

LUIZ
Your Grace, the halberdiers are mercenary people who stipulated for a trifle on account.

DUKE
How tiresome! Well, let us hope the Grand Inquisitor is a blind gentleman. And the band who were to have had the honour of escorting us? I see no band!

LUIZ
Your Grace, the band are sordid persons who required to be paid in advance.

DUCHESS
That's so like a band!

DUKE (annoyed)
Insuperable difficulties meet me at every turn!

DUCHESS
But surely they know His Grace?

LUIZ
Exactly—they know His Grace.

DUKE
Well, let us hope that the Grand Inquisitor is a deaf gentleman. A cornet-a-piston would be something. You do not happen to possess the accomplishment of tootling like a cornet-a-piston?

LUIZ
Alas, no, Your Grace! But I can imitate a farmyard.

DUKE (doubtfully).
I don't see how that would help us. I don't see how we could bring it in.

CASILDA
It would not help us in the least. We are not a parcel of graziers come to market, dolt!

(LUIZ rises.)

DUKE
My love, our suite's feelings! (To LUIZ.) Be so good as to ring the bell and inform the Grand Inquisitor that his Grace the Duke of Plaza-Toro, Count Matadoro, Baron Picadoro—

DUCHESS
And suite—

DUKE
And suite—have arrived at Venice, and seek—

CASILDA
Desire—

DUCHESS
Demand!

DUKE
And demand an audience.

LUIZ
Your Grace has but to command.

DUKE (much moved)
I felt sure of it—I felt sure of it!

(Exit LUIZ into Ducal Palace.)

And now, my love—(aside to DUCHESS) Shall we tell her? I think so—(aloud to CASILDA) And now, my love, prepare for a magnificent surprise. It is my agreeable duty to reveal to you a secret which should make you the happiest young lady in Venice!

CASILDA
A secret?

DUCHESS
A secret which, for State reasons, it has been necessary to preserve for twenty years.

DUKE
When you were a prattling babe of six months old you were married by proxy to no less a personage than the infant son and heir of His Majesty the immeasurably wealthy King of Barataria!

CASILDA
Married to the infant son of the King of Barataria?
Was I consulted? (Duke shakes his head.) Then it was a most unpardonable liberty!

DUKE
Consider his extreme youth and forgive him. Shortly after the ceremony that misguided monarch abandoned the creed of his forefathers, and became a Wesleyan Methodist of the most bigoted and persecuting type. The Grand Inquisitor, determined that the innovation should not be perpetuated in Barataria, caused your smiling and unconscious husband to be stolen and conveyed to Venice. A fortnight since the Methodist Monarch and all his Wesleyan Court were killed in an insurrection, and we

are here to ascertain the whereabouts of your husband, and to hail you, our daughter, as Her Majesty, the reigning Queen of Barataria!

(Kneels.)

(During this speech LUIZ re-enters.)

DUCHESS
Your Majesty!

(Kneels.)

(Drum roll.)

DUKE
It is at such moments as these that one feels how necessary it is to travel with a full band.

CASILDA
I, the Queen of Barataria! But I've nothing to wear!
We are practically penniless!

DUKE
That point has not escaped me. Although I am unhappily in straitened circumstances at present, my social influence is something enormous; and a Company, to be called the Duke of Plaza-Toro, Limited, is in course of formation to work me. An influential directorate has been secured, and I shall myself join the Board after allotment.

CASILDA
Am I to understand that the Queen of Barataria may be called upon at any time to witness her honoured sire in process of liquidation?

DUCHESS
The speculation is not exempt from that drawback. If your father should stop, it will, of course, be necessary to wind him up.

CASILDA
But it's so undignified—it's so degrading! A Grandee of Spain turned into a public company! Such a thing was never heard of!

DUKE
My child, the Duke of Plaza-Toro does not follow fashions—he leads them. He always leads everybody. When he was in the army he led his regiment. He occasionally led them into action. He invariably led them out of it.

SONG—**DUKE OF PLAZA-TORO**
In enterprise of martial kind,
When there was any fighting,
He led his regiment from behind—

He found it less exciting.
But when away his regiment ran,
His place was at the fore, O—
That celebrated,
Cultivated,
Underrated
Nobleman,
The Duke of Plaza-Toro!

ALL
In the first and foremost flight, ha, ha!
You always found that knight, ha, ha!
That celebrated,
Cultivated,
Underrated
Nobleman,
The Duke of Plaza-Toro!

DUKE
When, to evade Destruction's hand,
To hide they all proceeded,
No soldier in that gallant band
Hid half as well as he did.
He lay concealed throughout the war,
And so preserved his gore, O!
That unaffected,
Undetected,
Well-connected
Warrior,
The Duke of Plaza-Toro!

ALL
In every doughty deed, ha, ha!
He always took the lead, ha, ha!
That unaffected,
Undetected,
Well-connected
Warrior,
The Duke of Plaza-Toro!

DUKE
When told that they would all be shot
Unless they left the service,
That hero hesitated not,
So marvellous his nerve is.
He sent his resignation in,
The first of all his corps, O!
That very knowing,

Overflowing,
Easy-going
Paladin,
The Duke of Plaza-Toro!

ALL
To men of grosser clay, ha, ha!
He always showed the way, ha, ha!
That very knowing,
Overflowing,
Easy-going
Paladin,
The Duke of Plaza-Toro!

(Exeunt DUKE and DUCHESS into Grand Ducal Palace. As soon as they have disappeared, LUIZ and
CASILDA rush to each other's arms.)

RECITATIVE AND DUET—**CASILDA AND LUIZ.**
O rapture, when alone together
Two loving hearts and those that bear them
May join in temporary tether,
Though Fate apart should rudely tear them.

CASILDA
Necessity, Invention's mother,
Compelled me to a course of feigning—
But, left alone with one another,
I will atone for my disdaining!

AIR

CASILDA
Ah, well-beloved,
Mine angry frown
Is but a gown
That serves to dress
My gentleness!

LUIZ
Ah, well-beloved,
Thy cold disdain,
It gives no pain—
'Tis mercy, played
In masquerade!

BOTH
Ah, well-beloved, etc.

CASILDA
O Luiz, Luiz—what have you said? What have I done? What have I allowed you to do?

LUIZ
Nothing, I trust, that you will ever have reason to repent.

(Offering to embrace her.)

CASILDA (withdrawing from him)
Nay, Luiz, it may not be. I have embraced you for the last time.

LUIZ (amazed)
Casilda!

CASILDA
I have just learnt, to my surprise and indignation, that I was wed in babyhood to the infant son of the King of Barataria!

LUIZ
The son of the King of Barataria? The child who was stolen in infancy by the Inquisition?

CASILDA
The same. But, of course, you know his story.

LUIZ
Know his story? Why, I have often told you that my mother was the nurse to whose charge he was entrusted!

CASILDA
True. I had forgotten. Well, he has been discovered, and my father has brought me here to claim his hand.

LUIZ.
But you will not recognize this marriage? It took place when you were too young to understand its import.

CASILDA
Nay, Luiz, respect my principles and cease to torture me with vain entreaties. Henceforth my life is another's.

LUIZ
But stay—the present and the future—they are another's; but the past—that at least is ours, and none can take it from us. As we may revel in naught else, let us revel in that!

CASILDA
I don't think I grasp your meaning.

LUIZ
Yet it is logical enough. You say you cease to love me?

CASILDA (demurely)
I say I may not love you.

LUIZ
Ah, but you do not say you did not love me?

CASILDA
I loved you with a frenzy that words are powerless to express—and that but ten brief minutes since!

LUIZ
Exactly. My own—that is, until ten minutes since, my own—my lately loved, my recently adored—tell me that until, say a quarter of an hour ago, I was all in all to thee!

(Embracing her.)

CASILDA
I see your idea. It's ingenious, but don't do that.

(Releasing herself.)

LUIZ
There can be no harm in revelling in the past.

CASILDA
None whatever, but an embrace cannot be taken to act retrospectively.

LUIZ
Perhaps not!

CASILDA
We may recollect an embrace—I recollect many—but we must not repeat them.

LUIZ
Then let us recollect a few!

(A moment's pause, as they recollect, then both heave a deep sigh.)

LUIZ
Ah, Casilda, you were to me as the sun is to the earth!

CASILDA
A quarter of an hour ago?

LUIZ
About that.

CASILDA

And to think that, but for this miserable discovery, you would have been my own for life!

LUIZ

Through life to death—a quarter of an hour ago!

CASILDA

How greedily my thirsty ears would have drunk the golden melody of those sweet words a quarter—well, it's now about twenty minutes since.

(Looking at her watch.)

LUIZ

About that. In such a matter one cannot be too precise.

CASILDA

And now our love, so full of life, is but a silent, solemn memory!

LUIZ

Must it be so, Casilda?

CASILDA

Luiz, it must be so!

DUET—**CASILDA and LUIZ.**

LUIZ.
There was a time—
A time for ever gone—ah, woe is me!
It was no crime
To love but thee alone—ah, woe is me!
One heart, one life, one soul,
One aim, one goal—
Each in the other's thrall,
Each all in all, ah, woe is me!

BOTH
Oh, bury, bury—let the grave close o'er
The days that were—that never will be more!
Oh, bury, bury love that all condemn,
And let the whirlwind mourn its requiem!

CASILDA
Dead as the last year's leaves—
As gathered flowers—ah, woe is me!
Dead as the garnered sheaves,
That love of ours—ah, woe is me!

Born but to fade and die
When hope was high,
Dead and as far away
As yesterday!—ah, woe is me!

BOTH
Oh, bury, bury—let the grave close o'er, etc.

(Re-enter from the Ducal Palace the DUKE and DUCHESS, followed by DON ALHAMBRA DEL BOLERO, the Grand Inquisitor.)

DUKE
My child, allow me to present to you His Distinction Don Alhambra del Bolero, the Grand Inquisitor of Spain. It was His Distinction who so thoughtfully abstracted your infant husband and brought him to Venice.

DON ALHAMBRA DEL BOLERO
So this is the little lady who is so unexpectedly called upon to assume the functions of Royalty! And a very nice little lady, too!

DUKE
Jimp, isn't she?

DON ALHAMBRA DEL BOLERO
Distinctly jimp. Allow me! (Offers his hand. She turns away scornfully.) Naughty temper!

DUKE
You must make some allowance. Her Majesty's head is a little turned by her access of dignity.

DON ALHAMBRA DEL BOLERO
I could have wished that Her Majesty's access of dignity had turned it in this direction.

DUCHESS
Unfortunately, if I am not mistaken, there appears to be some little doubt as to His Majesty's whereabouts.

CASILDA (aside).
A doubt as to his whereabouts?
Then we may yet be saved!

DON ALHAMBRA DEL BOLERO
A doubt? Oh dear, no—no doubt at all! He is here, in Venice, plying the modest but picturesque calling of a gondolier. I can give you his address—I see him every day! In the entire annals of our history there is absolutely no circumstance so entirely free from all manner of doubt of any kind whatever! Listen, and I'll tell you all about it.

SONG—DON ALHAMBRA (with DUKE, DUCHESS, CASILDA, and LUIZ)
I stole the Prince, and I brought him here,

And left him gaily prattling
With a highly respectable gondolier,
Who promised the Royal babe to rear,
And teach him the trade of a timoneer
With his own beloved bratling.

Both of the babes were strong and stout,
And, considering all things, clever.
Of that there is no manner of doubt—
No probable, possible shadow of doubt—
No possible doubt whatever.

ALL
No possible doubt whatever.

But owing, I'm much disposed to fear,
To his terrible taste for tippling,
That highly respectable gondolier
Could never declare with a mind sincere
Which of the two was his offspring dear,
And which the Royal stripling!

Which was which he could never make out
Despite his best endeavour.
Of that there is no manner of doubt—
No probable, possible shadow of doubt—
No possible doubt whatever.

ALL
No possible doubt whatever.

Time sped, and when at the end of a year
I sought that infant cherished,
That highly respectable gondolier
Was lying a corpse on his humble bier—
I dropped a Grand Inquisitor's tear—
That gondolier had perished.

A taste for drink, combined with gout,
Had doubled him up for ever.
Of that there is no manner of doubt—
No probable, possible shadow of doubt—
No possible doubt whatever.

ALL
No possible doubt whatever.

The children followed his old career—

(This statement can't be parried)
Of a highly respectable gondolier:
Well, one of the two (who will soon be here)—
But which of the two is not quite clear—
Is the Royal Prince you married!

Search in and out and round about,
And you'll discover never
A tale so free from every doubt—
All probable, possible shadow of doubt—
All possible doubt whatever!

ALL.
A tale free from every doubt, etc.

CASILDA
Then do you mean to say that I am married to one of two gondoliers, but it is impossible to say which?

DON ALHAMBRA DEL BOLERO
Without any doubt of any kind whatever. But be reassured: the nurse to whom your husband was entrusted is the mother of the musical young man who is such a past-master of that delicately modulated instrument (indicating the drum). She can, no doubt, establish the King's identity beyond all question.

LUIZ.
Heavens, how did he know that?

DON ALHAMBRA DEL BOLERO
My young friend, a Grand Inquisitor is always up to date. (To CASILDA) His mother is at present the wife of a highly respectable and old-established brigand, who carries on an extensive practice in the mountains around Cordova. Accompanied by two of my emissaries, he will set off at once for his mother's address. She will return with them, and if she finds any difficulty in making up her mind, the persuasive influence of the torture chamber will jog her memory.

RECITATIVE—**CASILDA and DON ALHAMBRA.**

CASILDA
But, bless my heart, consider my position!
I am the wife of one, that's very clear;
But who can tell, except by intuition,
Which is the Prince, and which the Gondolier?

DON ALHAMBRA DEL BOLERO
Submit to Fate without unseemly wrangle:
Such complications frequently occur—
Life is one closely complicated tangle:
Death is the only true unraveller!

QUINTET—**DUKE, DUCHESS, CASILDA, LUIZ**, and **GRAND INQUISITOR.**

ALL
Try we life-long, we can never
Straighten out life's tangled skein,
Why should we, in vain endeavour,
Guess and guess and guess again?

LUIZ
Life's a pudding full of plums,

DUCHESS
Care's a canker that benumbs.

ALL
Life's a pudding full of plums,
Care's a canker that benumbs.
Wherefore waste our elocution
On impossible solution?
Life's a pleasant institution,
Let us take it as it comes!

Set aside the dull enigma,
We shall guess it all too soon;
Failure brings no kind of stigma—
Dance we to another tune!

LUIZ
String the lyre and fill the cup,

DUCHESS
Lest on sorrow we should sup.

ALL
Hop and skip to Fancy's fiddle,
Hands across and down the middle—
Life's perhaps the only riddle
That we shrink from giving up!

(Exeunt all into Ducal Palace except LUIZ, who goes off in gondola.)

(Enter GONDOLIERS and CONTADINE, followed by MARCO, GIANETTA, GIUSEPPE, and TESSA.)

CHORUS
Bridegroom and bride!
Knot that's insoluble,
Voices all voluble
Hail it with pride.

Bridegroom and bride!
We in sincerity
Wish you prosperity,
Bridegroom and bride!

SONG—**TESSA**

TESSA
When a merry maiden marries,
Sorrow goes and pleasure tarries;
Every sound becomes a song,
All is right, and nothing's wrong!
From to-day and ever after
Let our tears be tears of laughter.
Every sigh that finds a vent
Be a sigh of sweet content!
When you marry, merry maiden,
Then the air with love is laden;
Every flower is a rose,
Every goose becomes a swan,
Every kind of trouble goes
Where the last year's snows have gone!

CHORUS
Sunlight takes the place of shade
When you marry, merry maid!

TESSA
When a merry maiden marries,
Sorrow goes and pleasure tarries;
Every sound becomes a song,
All is right, and nothing's wrong.
Gnawing Care and aching Sorrow,
Get ye gone until to-morrow;
Jealousies in grim array,
Ye are things of yesterday!
When you marry, merry maiden,
Then the air with joy is laden;
All the corners of the earth
Ring with music sweetly played,
Worry is melodious mirth,
Grief is joy in masquerade;

CHORUS
Sullen night is laughing day—
All the year is merry May!

(At the end of the song, DON ALHAMBRA enters at back. The GONDOLIERS and CONTADINE shrink from him, and gradually go off, much alarmed.)

GIUSEPPE
And now our lives are going to begin in real earnest!
What's a bachelor? A mere nothing—he's a chrysalis. He can't be said to live—he exists.

MARCO
What a delightful institution marriage is! Why have we wasted all this time? Why didn't we marry ten years ago?

TESSA
Because you couldn't find anybody nice enough.

GIANETTA
Because you were waiting for us.

MARCO
I suppose that was the reason. We were waiting for you without knowing it. (DON ALHAMBRA comes forward.) Hallo!

DON ALHAMBRA DEL BOLERO
Good morning.

GIUSEPPE
If this gentleman is an undertaker it's a bad omen.

DON ALHAMBRA DEL BOLERO
Ceremony of some sort going on?

GIUSEPPE (aside)
He is an undertaker! (Aloud.) No—a little unimportant family gathering. Nothing in your line.

DON ALHAMBRA DEL BOLERO
Somebody's birthday, I suppose?

GIANETTA
Yes, mine!

TESSA
And mine!

MARCO
And mine!

GIUSEPPE
And mine!

DON ALHAMBRA DEL BOLERO
Curious coincidence! And how old may you all be?

TESSA
It's a rude question—but about ten minutes.

DON ALHAMBRA DEL BOLERO
Remarkably fine children! But surely you are jesting?

TESSA
In other words, we were married about ten minutes since.

DON ALHAMBRA DEL BOLERO
Married! You don't mean to say you are married?

MARCO
Oh yes, we are married.

DON ALHAMBRA DEL BOLERO
What, both of you?

ALL
All four of us.

DON ALHAMBRA DEL BOLERO (aside)
Bless my heart, how extremely awkward!

GIANETTA
You don't mind, I suppose?

TESSA
You were not thinking of either of us for yourself, I presume? Oh, Giuseppe, look at him—he was. He's heart-broken!

DON ALHAMBRA DEL BOLERO
No, no, I wasn't! I wasn't!

GIUSEPPE
Now, my man (slapping him on the back), we don't want anything in your line to-day, and if your curiosity's satisfied—you can go!

DON ALHAMBRA DEL BOLERO
You mustn't call me your man. It's a liberty. I don't think you know who I am.

GIUSEPPE
Not we, indeed! We are jolly gondoliers, the sons of Baptisto Palmieri, who led the last revolution. Republicans, heart and soul, we hold all men to be equal. As we abhor oppression, we abhor kings: as we detest vain-glory, we detest rank: as we despise effeminacy, we despise wealth. We are Venetian

gondoliers—your equals in everything except our calling, and in that at once your masters and your servants.

DON ALHAMBRA DEL BOLERO
Bless my heart, how unfortunate! One of you may be Baptisto's son, for anything I know to the contrary; but the other is no less a personage than the only son of the late King of Barataria.

ALL
What!

DON ALHAMBRA DEL BOLERO
And I trust—I trust it was that one who slapped me on the shoulder and called me his man!

GIUSEPPE
One of us a king!

MARCO
Not brothers!

TESSA
The King of Barataria!

[Together]

GIANETTA
Well, who'd have thought it!

MARCO
But which is it?

DON ALHAMBRA DEL BOLERO
What does it matter? As you are both Republicans, and hold kings in detestation, of course you'll abdicate at once. Good morning!

(Going.)

GIANETTA and TESSA
Oh, don't do that!

(MARCO and GIUSEPPE stop him.)

GIUSEPPE
Well, as to that, of course there are kings and kings.
When I say that I detest kings, I mean I detest bad kings.

DON ALHAMBRA DEL BOLERO
I see. It's a delicate distinction.

GIUSEPPE

Quite so. Now I can conceive a kind of king—an ideal king—the creature of my fancy, you know—who would be absolutely unobjectionable. A king, for instance, who would abolish taxes and make everything cheap, except gondolas—

MARCO

And give a great many free entertainments to the gondoliers—

GIUSEPPE

And let off fireworks on the Grand Canal, and engage all the gondolas for the occasion—

MARCO

And scramble money on the Rialto among the gondoliers.

GIUSEPPE

Such a king would be a blessing to his people, and if I were a king, that is the sort of king I would be.

MARCO

And so would I!

DON ALHAMBRA DEL BOLERO

Come, I'm glad to find your objections are not insuperable.

MARCO and GIUSEPPE

Oh, they're not insuperable.

GIANETTA and TESSA

No, they're not insuperable.

GIUSEPPE

Besides, we are open to conviction.

GIANETTA

Yes; they are open to conviction.

TESSA

Oh! they've often been convicted.

GIUSEPPE

Our views may have been hastily formed on insufficient grounds. They may be crude, ill-digested, erroneous. I've a very poor opinion of the politician who is not open to conviction.

TESSA (to GIANETTA)

Oh, he's a fine fellow!

GIANETTA

Yes, that's the sort of politician for my money!

DON ALHAMBRA DEL BOLERO
Then we'll consider it settled. Now, as the country is in a state of insurrection, it is absolutely necessary that you should assume the reins of Government at once; and, until it is ascertained which of you is to be king, I have arranged that you will reign jointly, so that no question can arise hereafter as to the validity of any of your acts.

MARCO
As one individual?

DON ALHAMBRA DEL BOLERO
As one individual.

GIUSEPPE (linking himself with MARCO)
Like this?

DON ALHAMBRA DEL BOLERO
Something like that.

MARCO
And we may take our friends with us, and give them places about the Court?

DON ALHAMBRA DEL BOLERO
Undoubtedly.
That's always done!

MARCO
I'm convinced!

GIUSEPPE
So am I!

TESSA
Then the sooner we're off the better.

GIANETTA
We'll just run home and pack up a few things (going)—

DON ALHAMBRA DEL BOLERO
Stop, stop—that won't do at all—ladies are not admitted.

ALL
What!

DON ALHAMBRA DEL BOLERO
Not admitted. Not at present. Afterwards, perhaps. We'll see.

GIUSEPPE
Why, you don't mean to say you are going to separate us from our wives!

DON ALHAMBRA DEL BOLERO (aside).
This is very awkward! (Aloud.) Only for a time—a few months. Alter all, what is a few months?

TESSA
But we've only been married half an hour!

(Weeps.)

FINALE, ACT I.

SONG—**GIANETTA**.
Kind sir, you cannot have the heart
Our lives to part
From those to whom an hour ago
We were united!
Before our flowing hopes you stem,
Ah, look at them,
And pause before you deal this blow,
All uninvited!
You men can never understand
That heart and hand
Cannot be separated when
We go a-yearning;
You see, you've only women's eyes
To idolize
And only women's hearts, poor men,
To set you burning!
Ah me, you men will never understand
That woman's heart is one with woman's hand!

Some kind of charm you seem to find
In womankind—
Some source of unexplained delight
(Unless you're jesting),
But what attracts you, I confess,
I cannot guess,
To me a woman's face is quite
Uninteresting!
If from my sister I were torn,
It could be borne—
I should, no doubt, be horrified,
But I could bear it;—
But Marco's quite another thing—
He is my King,
He has my heart and none beside
Shall ever share it!
Ah me, you men will never understand

That woman's heart is one with woman's hand!

RECITATIVE—**DON ALHAMBRA**.
Do not give way to this uncalled-for grief,
Your separation will be very brief.
To ascertain which is the King
And which the other,
To Barataria's Court I'll bring
His foster-mother;
Her former nurseling to declare
She'll be delighted.
That settled, let each happy pair
Be reunited.

MARCO, GIUSEPPE,
Viva! His argument is strong!

GIANETTA, TESSA
Viva! We'll not be parted long!
Viva! It will be settled soon!
Viva! Then comes our honeymoon!

(Exit DON ALHAMBRA.)

QUARTET—**MARCO, GIUSEPPE, GIANETTA, TESSA.**

GIANETTA
hen one of us will be a Queen,
And sit on a golden throne,
With a crown instead
Of a hat on her head,
And diamonds all her own!
With a beautiful robe of gold and green,
I've always understood;
I wonder whether
She'd wear a feather?
I rather think she should!

ALL
Oh, 'tis a glorious thing, I ween,
To be a regular Royal Queen!
No half-and-half affair, I mean,
But a right-down regular Royal Queen!

MARCO
She'll drive about in a carriage and pair,
With the King on her left-hand side,
And a milk-white horse,

As a matter of course,
Whenever she wants to ride!
With beautiful silver shoes to wear
Upon her dainty feet;
With endless stocks
Of beautiful frocks
And as much as she wants to eat!

ALL
Oh, 'tis a glorious thing, I ween, etc.

TESSA
Whenever she condescends to walk,
Be sure she'll shine at that,
With her haughty stare
And her nose in the air,
Like a well-born aristocrat!
At elegant high society talk
She'll bear away the bell,
With her "How de do?"
And her "How are you?"
And "I trust I see you well!"

ALL
Oh, 'tis a glorious thing, I ween, etc.

GIUSEPPE
And noble lords will scrape and bow,
And double themselves in two,
And open their eyes
In blank surprise
At whatever she likes to do.
And everybody will roundly vow
She's fair as flowers in May,
And say, "How clever!"
At whatsoever
She condescends to say!

ALL
Oh, 'tis a glorious thing, I ween,
To be a regular Royal Queen!
No half-and-half affair, I mean,
But a right-down regular Royal Queen!

(Enter CHORUS of GONDOLIERS and CONTADINE.)

CHORUS
Now, pray, what is the cause of this remarkable hilarity?

This sudden ebullition of unmitigated jollity?
Has anybody blessed you with a sample of his charity?
Or have you been adopted by a gentleman of quality?

MARCO and GIUSEPPE
Replying, we sing
As one individual,
As I find I'm a king,
To my kingdom I bid you all.
I'm aware you object
To pavilions and palaces,
But you'll find I respect
Your Republican fallacies.

CHORUS
As they know we object
To pavilions and palaces,
How can they respect
Our Republican fallacies?

MARCO and GIUSEPPE

MARCO
For every one who feels inclined,
Some post we undertake to find
Congenial with his frame of mind—
And all shall equal be.

GIUSEPPE
The Chancellor in his peruke—
The Earl, the Marquis, and the Dook,
The Groom, the Butler, and the Cook—
They all shall equal be.

MARCO
The Aristocrat who banks with Coutts—
The Aristocrat who hunts and shoots—
The Aristocrat who cleans our boots—
They all shall equal be!

GIUSEPPE
The Noble Lord who rules the State—
The Noble Lord who cleans the plate—

MARCO
The Noble Lord who scrubs the grate—
They all shall equal be!

GIUSEPPE

The Lord High Bishop orthodox—
The Lord High Coachman on the box—

MARCO

The Lord High Vagabond in the stocks—
They all shall equal be!

BOTH

For every one, etc.

Sing high, sing low,
Wherever they go,
They all shall equal be!

CHORUS

Sing high, sing low,
Wherever they go,
They all shall equal be!

The Earl, the Marquis, and the Dook,
The Groom, the Butler, and the Cook,
The Aristocrat who banks with Coutts,
The Aristocrat who cleans the boots,
The Noble Lord who rules the State,
The Noble Lord who scrubs the grate,
The Lord High Bishop orthodox,
The Lord High Vagabond in the stocks—

For every one, etc.

Sing high, sing low,
Wherever they go,
They all shall equal be!

Then hail! O King,
Whichever you may be,
To you we sing,
But do not bend the knee.
Then hail! O King.

MARCO and GIUSEPPE (together)

Come, let's away—our island crown awaits me—
Conflicting feelings rend my soul apart!
The thought of Royal dignity elates me,
But leaving thee behind me breaks my heart!

(Addressing GIANETTA and TESSA)

GIANETTA and TESSA (together)
Farewell, my love; on board you must be getting;
But while upon the sea you gaily roam,
Remember that a heart for thee is fretting—
The tender little heart you've left at home!

GIANETTA
Now, Marco dear,
My wishes hear:
While you're away
It's understood
You will be good
And not too gay.
To every trace
Of maiden grace
You will be blind,
And will not glance
By any chance
On womankind!

If you are wise,
You'll shut your eyes
Till we arrive,
And not address
A lady less
Than forty-five.
You'll please to frown
On every gown
That you may see;
And, O my pet,
You won't forget
You've married me!

And O my darling, O my pet,
Whatever else you may forget,
In yonder isle beyond the sea,
Do not forget you've married me!

TESSA
You'll lay your head
Upon your bed
At set of sun.
You will not sing
Of anything
To any one.
You'll sit and mope
All day, I hope,

And shed a tear
Upon the life
Your little wife
Is passing here.

And if so be
You think of me,
Please tell the moon!
I'll read it all
In rays that fall
On the lagoon:
You'll be so kind
As tell the wind
How you may be,
And send me words
By little birds
To comfort me!

And O my darling, O my pet,
Whatever else you may forget,
In yonder isle beyond the sea,
Do not forget you've married me!

QUARTET
Oh my darling, O my pet, etc.

CHORUS (during which a "Xebeque" is hauled alongside the quay)
Then away we go to an island fair
That lies in a Southern sea:
We know not where, and we don't much care,
Wherever that isle may be.

THE MEN (hauling on boat)
One, two, three,
Haul!
One, two, three,
Haul!
One, two, three,
Haul!
With a will!

ALL
When the breezes are a-blowing
The ship will be going,
When they don't we shall all stand still!
Then away we go to an island fair,
We know not where, and we don't much care,
Wherever that isle may be.

SOLO—**MARCO**
Away we go
To a balmy isle,
Where the roses blow
All the winter while.

ALL (hoisting sail)
Then away we go to an island fair
That lies in a Southern sea:
Then away we go to an island fair,
Then away, then away, then away!

(The men embark on the "Xebeque." MARCO and GIUSEPPE embracing GIANETTA and TESSA. The girls wave a farewell to the men as the curtain falls.)

END OF ACT I

ACT II

SCENE.—Pavilion in the Court of Barataria. MARCO and GIUSEPPE, magnificently dressed, are seated on two thrones, occupied in cleaning the crown and the sceptre. The GONDOLIERS are discovered, dressed, some as courtiers, officers of rank, etc., and others as private soldiers and servants of various degrees. All are enjoying themselves without reference to social distinctions—some playing cards, others throwing dice, some reading, others playing cup and ball, "morra", etc.

CHORUS of MEN with MARCO and GIUSEPPE
Of happiness the very pith
In Barataria you may see:
A monarchy that's tempered with
Republican Equality.
This form of government we find
The beau ideal of its kind—
A despotism strict combined
With absolute equality!

MARCO and GIUSEPPE
Two kings, of undue pride bereft,
Who act in perfect unity,
Whom you can order right and left
With absolute impunity.
Who put their subjects at their ease
By doing all they can to please!
And thus, to earn their bread-and-cheese,
Seize every opportunity.

CHORUS
Of happiness the very pith, etc.

MARCO
Gentlemen, we are much obliged to you for your expressions of satisfaction and good feeling—I say, we are much obliged to you for your expressions of satisfaction and good feeling.

ALL
We heard you.

MARCO
We are delighted, at any time, to fall in with sentiments so charmingly expressed.

ALL
That's all right.

GIUSEPPE
At the same time there is just one little grievance that we should like to ventilate.

ALL (angrily)
What?

GIUSEPPE
Don't be alarmed—it's not serious. It is arranged that, until it is decided which of us two is the actual King, we are to act as one person.

GIORGIO
Exactly.

GIUSEPPE
Now, although we act as one person, we are, in point of fact, two persons.

ANNIBALE
Ah, I don't think we can go into that. It is a legal fiction, and legal fictions are solemn things. Situated as we are, we can't recognize two independent responsibilities.

GIUSEPPE
No; but you can recognize two independent appetites. It's all very well to say we act as one person, but when you supply us with only one ration between us, I should describe it as a legal fiction carried a little too far.

ANNIBALE
It's rather a nice point. I don't like to express an opinion off-hand. Suppose we reserve it for argument before the full Court?

MARCO
Yes, but what are we to do in the meantime?

MARCO and GIUSEPPE

We want our tea.

ANNIBALE

I think we may make an interim order for double rations on their Majesties entering into the usual undertaking to indemnify in the event of an adverse decision?

GIORGIO

That, I think, will meet the case. But you must work hard—stick to it—nothing like work.

GIUSEPPE

Oh, certainly. We quite understand that a man who holds the magnificent position of King should do something to justify it. We are called "Your Majesty"; we are allowed to buy ourselves magnificent clothes; our subjects frequently nod to us in the streets; the sentries always return our salutes; and we enjoy the inestimable privilege of heading the subscription lists to all the principal charities. In return for these advantages the least we can do is to make ourselves useful about the Palace.

SONG—**GIUSEPPE with CHORUS**

Rising early in the morning,
We proceed to light the fire,
Then our Majesty adorning
In its workaday attire,
We embark without delay
On the duties of the day.

First, we polish off some batches
Of political despatches,
And foreign politicians circumvent;
Then, if business isn't heavy,
We may hold a Royal levee,
Or ratify some Acts of Parliament.
Then we probably review the household troops—
With the usual "Shalloo humps!" and "Shalloo hoops!"
Or receive with ceremonial and state
An interesting Eastern potentate.
After that we generally
Go and dress our private valet—
(It's a rather nervous duty—he's a touchy little man)—
Write some letters literary
For our private secretary—
He is shaky in his spelling, so we help him if we can.
Then, in view of cravings inner,
We go down and order dinner;
Then we polish the Regalia and the Coronation Plate—
Spend an hour in titivating
All our Gentlemen-in-Waiting;
Or we run on little errands for the Ministers of State.

Oh, philosophers may sing
Of the troubles of a King;
Yet the duties are delightful, and the privileges great;
But the privilege and pleasure
That we treasure beyond measure
Is to run on little errands for the Ministers of State.

CHORUS
Oh, philosophers may sing, etc.
After luncheon (making merry
On a bun and glass of sherry),
If we've nothing in particular to do,
We may make a Proclamation,
Or receive a deputation—
Then we possibly create a Peer or two.
Then we help a fellow-creature on his path
With the Garter or the Thistle or the Bath,
Or we dress and toddle off in semi-state
To a festival, a function, or a fete.
Then we go and stand as sentry
At the Palace (private entry),
Marching hither, marching thither, up and down and to and fro,
While the warrior on duty
Goes in search of beer and beauty
(And it generally happens that he hasn't far to go).
He relieves us, if he's able,
Just in time to lay the table,
Then we dine and serve the coffee, and at half-past twelve or one,
With a pleasure that's emphatic,
We retire to our attic
With the gratifying feeling that our duty has been done!

Oh, philosophers may sing
Of the troubles of a King,
But of pleasures there are many and of worries there are none;
And the culminating pleasure
That we treasure beyond measure
Is the gratifying feeling that our duty has been done!

CHORUS
Oh, philosophers may sing, etc.

(Exeunt all but MARCO and GIUSEPPF)

GIUSEPPE

Yes, it really is a very pleasant existence. They're all so singularly kind and considerate. You don't find them wanting to do this, or wanting to do that, or saying "It's my turn now." No, they let us have all the fun to ourselves, and never seem to grudge it.

MARCO
It makes one feel quite selfish. It almost seems like taking advantage of their good nature.

GIUSEPPE
How nice they were about the double rations.

MARCO
Most considerate. Ah! there's only one thing wanting to make us thoroughly comfortable.

GIUSEPPE
And that is?

MARCO
The dear little wives we left behind us three months ago.

GIUSEPPE
Yes, it is dull without female society. We can do without everything else, but we can't do without that.

MARCO
And if we have that in perfection, we have everything.
There is only one recipe for perfect happiness.

SONG—**MARCO**
Take a pair of sparkling eyes,
Hidden, ever and anon,
In a merciful eclipse—
Do not heed their mild surprise—
Having passed the Rubicon,
Take a pair of rosy lips;
Take a figure trimly planned—
Such as admiration whets—
(Be particular in this);
Take a tender little hand,
Fringed with dainty fingerettes,
Press it—in parenthesis;—
Ah! Take all these, you lucky man—
Take and keep them, if you can!

Take a pretty little cot—
Quite a miniature affair—
Hung about with trellised vine,
Furnish it upon the spot
With the treasures rich and rare
I've endeavoured to define.

Live to love and love to live—
You will ripen at your ease,
Growing on the sunny side—
Fate has nothing more to give.
You're a dainty man to please
If you are not satisfied.
Ah! Take my counsel, happy man;
Act upon it, if you can!

(Enter CHORUS of CONTADINE, running in, led by FIAMETTA and VITTORIA. They are met by all the Ex-
GONDOLIERS, who welcome them heartily.)

SCENE—**CHORUS OF GIRLS, QUARTET, DUET and CHORUS.**

Here we are, at the risk of our lives,
From ever so far, and we've brought your wives—
And to that end we've crossed the main,
And don't intend to return again!

FIAMETTA
Though obedience is strong,
Curiosity's stronger—
We waited for long,
Till we couldn't wait longer.

VITTORIA
It's imprudent, we know,
But without your society
Existence was slow,
And we wanted variety—

BOTH
Existence was slow, and we wanted variety.

ALL
So here we are, at the risk of our lives,
From ever so far, and we've brought your wives—
And to that end we've crossed the main,
And don't intend to return again!

(Enter GIANETTA and TESSA. They rush to the arms of MARCO and GIUSEPPE)

GIUSEPPE
Tessa!

TESSA
Giuseppe!

{All embrace.}

GIANETTA
Marco!

MARCO
Gianetta!

TESSA and GIANETTA

TESSA
After sailing to this island—

GIANETTA
Tossing in a manner frightful,

TESSA
We are all once more on dry land—

GIANETTA
And we find the change delightful,

TESSA
As at home we've been remaining—
We've not seen you both for ages,

GIANETTA
Tell me, are you fond of reigning?—
How's the food, and what's the wages?

TESSA
Does your new employment please ye?—

GIANETTA
How does Royalizing strike you?

TESSA
 Is it difficult or easy?—

GIANETTA
Do you think your subjects like you?

TESSA
I am anxious to elicit,
Is it plain and easy steering?

GIANETTA
Take it altogether, is it

Better fun than gondoliering?

BOTH
We shall both go on requesting
Till you tell us, never doubt it;
Everything is interesting,
Tell us, tell us all about it!

CHORUS
They will both go on requesting, etc.

TESSA
Is the populace exacting?

GIANETTA
Do they keep you at a distance?

TESSA
All unaided are you acting,

GIANETTA
Or do they provide assistance?

TESSA
When you're busy, have you got to
Get up early in the morning?

GIANETTA
If you do what you ought not to,
Do they give the usual warning?

TESSA
With a horse do they equip you?

GIANETTA
Lots of trumpeting and drumming?

TESSA
Do the Royal tradesmen tip you?

GIANETTA
Ain't the livery becoming!

TESSA
Does your human being inner
Feed on everything that nice is?

GIANETTA

Do they give you wine for dinner;
Peaches, sugar-plums, and ices?

BOTH
We shall both go on requesting
Till you tell us, never doubt it;
Everything is interesting,
Tell us, tell us all about it!

CHORUS
They will both go on requesting, etc.

MARCO
This is indeed a most delightful surprise!

TESSA
Yes, we thought you'd like it. You see, it was like this. After you left we felt very dull and mopey, and the days crawled by, and you never wrote; so at last I said to Gianetta, "I can't stand this any longer; those two poor Monarchs haven't got any one to mend their stockings or sew on their buttons or patch their clothes—at least, I hope they haven't—let us all pack up a change and go and see how they're getting on." And she said, "Done," and they all said, "Done"; and we asked old Giacopo to lend us his boat, and he said, "Done"; and we've crossed the sea, and, thank goodness, that's done; and here we are, and—and—I've done!

GIANETTA
And now—which of you is King?

TESSA
And which of us is Queen?

GIUSEPPE
That we shan't know until Nurse turns up. But never mind that—the question is, how shall we celebrate the commencement of our honeymoon? Gentlemen, will you allow us to offer you a magnificent banquet?

ALL
We will!

GIUSEPPE
Thanks very much; and, ladies, what do you say to a dance?

TESSA
A banquet and a dance! O, it's too much happiness!

CHORUS and DANCE
Dance a cachucha, fandango, bolero,
Xeres we'll drink—Manzanilla, Montero—
Wine, when it runs in abundance, enhances

The reckless delight of that wildest of dances!
To the pretty pitter-pitter-patter,
And the clitter-clitter-clitter-clatter—
Clitter—clitter—clatter,
Pitter—pitter—patter,
Patter, patter, patter, patter, we'll dance.
Old Xeres we'll drink—Manzanilla, Montero;
For wine, when it runs in abundance, enhances
The reckless delight of that wildest of dances!

(Cachucha.)

(The dance is interrupted by the unexpected appearance of DON ALHAMBRA, who looks on with astonishment. MARCO and GIUSEPPE appear embarrassed. The others run off, except DRUMMER BOY, who is driven off by DON ALHAMBRA)

DON ALHAMBRA DEL BOLERO
Good evening. Fancy ball?

GIUSEPPE
No, not exactly. A little friendly dance. That's all. Sorry you're late.

DON ALHAMBRA DEL BOLERO
But I saw a groom dancing, and a footman!

MARCO
Yes. That's the Lord High Footman.

DON ALHAMBRA DEL BOLERO
And, dear me, a common little drummer boy!

GIUSEPPE
Oh no!
That's the Lord High Drummer Boy.

DON ALHAMBRA DEL BOLERO
But surely, surely the servants'-hall is the place for these gentry?

GIUSEPPE
Oh dear no! We have appropriated the servants'-hall. It's the Royal Apartment, and accessible only by tickets obtainable at the Lord Chamberlain's office.

MARCO
We really must have some place that we can call our own.

DON ALHAMBRA DEL BOLERO (puzzled).
I'm afraid I'm not quite equal to the intellectual pressure of the conversation.

GIUSEPPE
You see, the Monarchy has been re-modelled on Republican principles.

DON ALHAMBRA DEL BOLERO
What!

GIUSEPPE
All departments rank equally, and everybody is at the head of his department.

DON ALHAMBRA DEL BOLERO
I see.

MARCO
I'm afraid you're annoyed.

DON ALHAMBRA DEL BOLERO
No. I won't say that. It's not quite what I expected.

GIUSEPPE
I'm awfully sorry.

MARCO
So am I.

GIUSEPPE
By the by, can I offer you anything after your voyage?
A plate of macaroni and a rusk?

DON ALHAMBRA DEL BOLERO (preoccupied).
No, no—nothing—nothing.

GISEPPE
Obliged to be careful?

DON ALHAMBRA DEL BOLERO
Yes—gout. You see, in every Court there are distinctions that must be observed.

GIUSEPPE (puzzled).
There are, are there?

DON ALHAMBRA DEL BOLERO
Why, of course. For instance, you wouldn't have a Lord High Chancellor play leapfrog with his own cook.

MARCO
Why not?

DON ALHAMBRA DEL BOLERO
Why not! Because a Lord High Chancellor is a personage of great dignity, who should never, under any

circumstances, place himself in the position of being told to tuck in his tuppenny, except by noblemen of his own rank. A Lord High Archbishop, for instance, might tell a Lord High Chancellor to tuck in his tuppenny, but certainly not a cook, gentlemen, certainly not a cook.

GIUSEPPE
Not even a Lord High Cook?

DON ALHAMBRA DEL BOLERO
My good friend, that is a rank that is not recognized at the Lord Chamberlain's office. No, no, it won't do. I'll give you an instance in which the experiment was tried.

SONG—**DON ALHAMBRA, with MARCO and GIUSEPPE**

DON ALHAMBRA DEL BOLERO
There lived a King, as I've been told,
In the wonder-working days of old,
When hearts were twice as good as gold,
And twenty times as mellow.
Good-temper triumphed in his face,
And in his heart he found a place
For all the erring human race
And every wretched fellow.
When he had Rhenish wine to drink
It made him very sad to think
That some, at junket or at jink,
Must be content with toddy.

MARCO and GIUSEPPE
With toddy, must be content with toddy.

DON ALHAMBRA DEL BOLERO
He wished all men as rich as he
(And he was rich as rich could be),
So to the top of every tree
Promoted everybody.

MARCO and GIUSEPPE
Now, that's the kind of King for me.
He wished all men as rich as he,
So to the top of every tree
Promoted everybody!

DON ALHAMBRA DEL BOLERO
Lord Chancellors were cheap as sprats,
And Bishops in their shovel hats
Were plentiful as tabby cats—
In point of fact, too many.
Ambassadors cropped up like hay,

Prime Ministers and such as they
Grew like asparagus in May,
And Dukes were three a penny.
On every side Field-Marshals gleamed,
Small beer were Lords-Lieutenant deemed,
With Admirals the ocean teemed
All round his wide dominions.

MARCO and GIUSEPPE
With Admirals all round his wide dominions.

DON ALHAMBRA DEL BOLERO
And Party Leaders you might meet
In twos and threes in every street
Maintaining, with no little heat,
Their various opinions.

MARCO and GIUSEPPE
Now that's a sight you couldn't beat—
Two Party Leaders in each street
Maintaining, with no little heat,
Their various opinions.

DON ALHAMBRA DEL BOLERO
That King, although no one denies
His heart was of abnormal size,
Yet he'd have acted otherwise
If he had been acuter.
The end is easily foretold,
When every blessed thing you hold
Is made of silver, or of gold,
You long for simple pewter.
When you have nothing else to wear
But cloth of gold and satins rare,
For cloth of gold you cease to care—
Up goes the price of shoddy.

MARCO and GIUSEPPE
Of shoddy, up goes the price of shoddy.

DON ALHAMBRA DEL BOLERO
In short, whoever you may be,
To this conclusion you'll agree,
When every one is somebodee,
Then no one's anybody!

MARCO and GIUSEPPE
Now that's as plain as plain can be,

To this conclusion we agree—

ALL
When every one is somebodee,
Then no one's anybody!

(GIANETTA and TESSA enter unobserved. The two girls, impelled by curiosity, remain listening at the back of the stage.)

DON ALHAMBRA DEL BOLERO
And now I have some important news to communicate. His Grace the Duke of Plaza-Toro, Her Grace the Duchess, and their beautiful daughter Casilda—I say their beautiful daughter Casilda—

GIUSEPPE
We heard you.

DON ALHAMBRA DEL BOLERO
Have arrived at Barataria, and may be here at any moment.

MARCO
The Duke and Duchess are nothing to us.

DON ALHAMBRA DEL BOLERO
But the daughter—the beautiful daughter! Aha!
Oh, you're a lucky dog, one of you!

GIUSEPPE
I think you're a very incomprehensible old gentleman.

DON ALHAMBRA DEL BOLERO
Not a bit—I'll explain. Many years ago when you (whichever you are) were a baby, you (whichever you are) were married to a little girl who has grown up to be the most beautiful young lady in Spain. That beautiful young lady will be here to claim you (whichever you are) in half an hour, and I congratulate that one (whichever it is) with all my heart.

MARCO
Married when a baby!

GIUSEPPE
But we were married three months ago!

DON ALHAMBRA DEL BOLERO
One of you—only one. The other (whichever it is) is an unintentional bigamist.

GIANETTA and TESSA (coming forward)
Well, upon my word!

DON ALHAMBRA DEL BOLERO

Eh?
Who are these young people?

TESSA
Who are we? Why, their wives, of course. We've just arrived.

DON ALHAMBRA DEL BOLERO
Their wives! Oh dear, this is very unfortunate!
Oh dear, this complicates matters! Dear, dear, what will Her
Majesty say?

GIANETTA
And do you mean to say that one of these Monarchs was already married?

TESSA
And that neither of us will be a Queen?

DON ALHAMBRA DEL BOLERO
That is the idea I intended to convey.

(TESSA and GIANETTA begin to cry.)

GIUSEPPE (to TESSA)
Tessa, my dear, dear child—

TESSA
Get away! perhaps it's you!

MARCO (to GIANETTA)
My poor, poor little woman!

GIANETTA
Don't! Who knows whose husband you are?

TESSA
And pray, why didn't you tell us all about it before they left Venice?

DON ALHAMBRA DEL BOLERO
Because, if I had, no earthly temptation would have induced these gentlemen to leave two such
extremely fascinating and utterly irresistible little ladies!

TESSA
There's something in that.

DON ALHAMBRA DEL BOLERO
I may mention that you will not be kept long in suspense, as the old lady who nursed the Royal child is at
present in the torture chamber, waiting for me to interview her.

GIUSEPPE
Poor old girl. Hadn't you better go and put her out of her suspense?

DON ALHAMBRA DEL BOLERO
Oh no—there's no hurry—she's all right. She has all the illustrated papers. However, I'll go and interrogate her, and, in the meantime, may I suggest the absolute propriety of your regarding yourselves as single young ladies. Good evening!

(Exit DON ALHAMBRA)

GIANETTA
Well, here's a pleasant state of things!

MARCO
Delightful. One of us is married to two young ladies, and nobody knows which; and the other is married to one young lady whom nobody can identify!

GIANETTA
And one of us is married to one of you, and the other is married to nobody.

TESSA
But which of you is married to which of us, and what's to become of the other?

(About to cry.)

GIUSEPPE
It's quite simple. Observe. Two husbands have managed to acquire three wives. Three wives—two husbands. (Reckoning up.) That's two-thirds of a husband to each wife.

TESSA
O Mount Vesuvius, here we are in arithmetic! My good sir, one can't marry a vulgar fraction!

GIUSEPPE
You've no right to call me a vulgar fraction.

MARCO
We are getting rather mixed. The situation is entangled. Let's try and comb it out.

QUARTET—**MARCO, GIUSEPPE, GIANETTA, TESSA**
In a contemplative fashion,
And a tranquil frame of mind,
Free from every kind of passion,
Some solution let us find.
Let us grasp the situation,
Solve the complicated plot—
Quiet, calm deliberation
Disentangles every knot.

TESSA, THE OTHERS.
I, no doubt, Giuseppe wedded— In a contemplative fashion
That's, of course, a slice of luck etc.
He is rather dunder-headed.
Still distinctly, he's a duck.

GIANETTA
I, a victim, too, of Cupid,

THE OTHERS
Let us grasp the
Marco married - that is clear situation, etc.
He's particularly stupid,
Still distinctly, he's a dear.

MARCO, THE OTHERS
To Gianetta I was mated; In a contemplative fashion
I can prove it in a trice: etc.
Though her charms are overrated,
Still I own she's rather nice.

GIUSEPPE, THE OTHERS
I to Tessa, willy-nilly, Let us grasp the situation
All at once a victim fell. etc.
She is what is called a silly,
Still she answers pretty well.

MARCO
Now when we were pretty babies
Some one married us, that's clear—

GIANETTA
And if I can catch her
I'll pinch her and scratch her
And send her away with a flea in her ear.

GIUSEPPE
He whom that young lady married,
To receive her can't refuse.

TESSA
If I overtake her
I'll warrant I'll make her
To shake in her aristocratical shoes!

GIANETTA (to TESSA)
If she married your Giuseppe
You and he will have to part—

TESSA (to GIANETTA)
If I have to do it
I'll warrant she'll rue it—
I'll teach her to marry the man of my heart!

If she married Messer Marco
You're a spinster, that is plain—

GIANETTA (to TESSA)
No matter—no matter.
If I can get at her
I doubt if her mother will know her again!

ALL
Quiet, calm deliberation
Disentangles every knot!

(Exeunt, pondering.)

(March. Enter procession of RETAINERS, heralding approach of DUKE, DUCHESS, and CASILDA. All three are now dressed with the utmost magnificence.)

CHORUS OF MEN, with DUKE and DUCHESS
With ducal pomp and ducal pride
(Announce these comers,
O ye kettle-drummers!)
Comes Barataria's high-born bride.
(Ye sounding cymbals clang!)
She comes to claim the Royal hand—
(Proclaim their Graces,
O ye double basses!)
Of the King who rules this goodly land.
(Ye brazen brasses bang!)

DUKE and DUCHESS
This polite attention touches
Heart of Duke and heart of Duchess
Who resign their pet
With profound regret.
She of beauty was a model
When a tiny tiddle-toddle,
And at twenty-one
She's excelled by none!

CHORUS
With ducal pomp and ducal pride, etc.

DUKE (to his ATTENDANTS)
Be good enough to inform His Majesty that His Grace the Duke of Plaza-Toro, Limited, has arrived, and begs—

CASILDA
Desires—

DUCHESS
Demands—

DUKE
And demands an audience. (Exeunt attendants.) And now, my child, prepare to receive the husband to whom you were united under such interesting and romantic circumstances.

CASILDA
But which is it? There are two of them!

DUKE
It is true that at present His Majesty is a double gentleman; but as soon as the circumstances of his marriage are ascertained, he will, ipso facto, boil down to a single gentleman—thus presenting a unique example of an individual who becomes a single man and a married man by the same operation.

DUCHESS (severely)
I have known instances in which the characteristics of both conditions existed concurrently in the same individual.

DUKE
Ah, he couldn't have been a Plaza-Toro.

DUCHESS
Oh! couldn't he, though!

CASILDA
Well, whatever happens, I shall, of course, be a dutiful wife, but I can never love my husband.

DUKE
I don't know. It's extraordinary what unprepossessing people one can love if one gives one's mind to it.

DUCHESS
I loved your father.

DUKE
My love—that remark is a little hard, I think?
Rather cruel, perhaps? Somewhat uncalled-for, I venture to believe?

DUCHESS
It was very difficult, my dear; but I said to myself, "That man is a Duke, and I will love him." Several of my relations bet me I couldn't, but I did—desperately!

SONG—**DUCHESS.**

On the day when I was wedded
To your admirable sire,
I acknowledge that I dreaded
An explosion of his ire.
I was overcome with panic—
For his temper was volcanic,
And I didn't dare revolt,
For I feared a thunderbolt!
I was always very wary,
For his fury was ecstatic—
His refined vocabulary
Most unpleasantly emphatic.
To the thunder
Of this Tartar
I knocked under
Like a martyr;
When intently
He was fuming,
I was gently
Unassuming—
When reviling
Me completely,
I was smiling
Very sweetly:
Giving him the very best, and getting back the very worst—
That is how I tried to tame your great progenitor—at first!
But I found that a reliance
On my threatening appearance,
And a resolute defiance
Of marital interference,
And a gentle intimation
Of my firm determination
To see what I could do
To be wife and husband too
Was the only thing required
For to make his temper supple,
And you couldn't have desired
A more reciprocating couple.
Ever willing
To be wooing,
We were billing—
We were cooing;
When I merely
From him parted,
We were nearly
Broken-hearted—

When in sequel
Reunited,
We were equally delighted.
So with double-shotted guns and colours nailed unto the mast,
I tamed your insignificant progenitor—at last!

CASILDA
My only hope is that when my husband sees what a shady family he has married into he will repudiate the contract altogether.

DUKE
Shady? A nobleman shady, who is blazing in the lustre of unaccustomed pocket-money? A nobleman shady, who can look back upon ninety-five quarterings? It is not every nobleman who is ninety-five quarters in arrear—I mean, who can look back upon ninety-five of them! And this, just as I have been floated at a premium! Oh fie!

DUCHESS
Your Majesty is surely unaware that directly your Majesty's father came before the public he was applied for over and over again.

DUKE
My dear, Her Majesty's father was in the habit of being applied for over and over again—and very urgently applied for, too—long before he was registered under the Limited Liability Act.

RECITATIVE—**DUKE**
To help unhappy commoners, and add to their enjoyment,
Affords a man of noble rank congenial employment;
Of our attempts we offer you examples illustrative:
The work is light, and, I may add, it's most remunerative.

DUET—**DUKE and DUCHESS**.

DUKE
Small titles and orders
For Mayors and Recorders
I get—and they're highly delighted—

DUCHESS
They're highly delighted!

DUKE
M.P.'s baronetted,
Sham Colonels gazetted,
And second-rate Aldermen knighted—

DUCHESS
Yes, Aldermen knighted.

DUKE
Foundation-stone laying
I find very paying:
It adds a large sum to my makings—

DUCHESS
Large sums to his makings.

DUKE
At charity dinners
The best of speech-spinners,
I get ten per cent on the takings—

DUCHESS
One-tenth of the takings.

DUCHESS
I present any lady
Whose conduct is shady
Or smacking of doubtful propriety—

DUKE
Doubtful propriety.

DUCHESS
When Virtue would quash her,
I take and whitewash her,
And launch her in first-rate society—

DUKE
First-rate society!

DUCHESS
I recommend acres
Of clumsy dressmakers—
Their fit and their finishing touches—

DUKE
Their finishing touches.

DUCHESS
A sum in addition
They pay for permission
To say that they make for the Duchess—

DUKE
They make for the Duchess!

DUKE
Those pressing prevailers,
The ready-made tailors,
Quote me as their great double-barrel—

DUCHESS
Their great double-barrel—

DUKE
I allow them to do so,
Though Robinson Crusoe
Would jib at their wearing apparel—

DUCHESS
Such wearing apparel!

DUKE
I sit, by selection,
Upon the direction
Of several Companies bubble—

DUCHESS
All Companies bubble!

DUKE
As soon as they're floated
I'm freely bank-noted—
I'm pretty well paid for my trouble—

DUCHESS
He's paid for his trouble!
At middle-class party
I play at ecarte—
And I'm by no means a beginner—

DUKE (significantly).
She's not a beginner.

DUCHESS
To one of my station
The remuneration—
Five guineas a night and my dinner—

DUKE
And wine with her dinner.

DUCHESS
I write letters blatant

On medicines patent—
And use any other you mustn't—

DUKE
Believe me, you mustn't—

DUCHESS
And vow my complexion
Derives its perfection
From somebody's soap—which it doesn't—

DUKE (significantly)
 It certainly doesn't!

DUKE
We're ready as witness
To any one's fitness
To fill any place or preferment—

DUCHESS
A place or preferment.

DUCHESS
We're often in waiting
At junket or feting,
And sometimes attend an interment—

DUKE
We enjoy an interment.

BOTH
In short, if you'd kindle
The spark of a swindle,
Lure simpletons into your clutches—
Yes; into your clutches.
Or hoodwink a debtor,
You cannot do better

DUCHESS
Than trot out a Duke or a Duchess—

DUKE
A Duke or a Duchess!

(Enter MARCO and GIUSEPPE)

DUKE
Ah! Their Majesties. Your Majesty!

(Bows with great ceremony.)

MARCO
The Duke of Plaza-Toro, I believe?

DUKE
The same

(MARCO and GIUSEPPE offer to shake hands with him. The DUKE bows ceremoniously. They endeavour to imitate him.)

Allow me to present—

GIUSEPPE
The young lady one of us married?

(MARCO and GIUSEPPE offer to shake hands with her. CASILDA curtsies formally. They endeavour to imitate her.)

CASILDA
Gentlemen, I am the most obedient servant of one of you. (Aside.) Oh, Luiz!

DUKE
I am now about to address myself to the gentleman whom my daughter married; the other may allow his attention to wander if he likes, for what I am about to say does not concern him. Sir, you will find in this young lady a combination of excellences which you would search for in vain in any young lady who had not the good fortune to be my daughter. There is some little doubt as to which of you is the gentleman I am addressing, and which is the gentleman who is allowing his attention to wander; but when that doubt is solved, I shall say (still addressing the attentive gentleman), "Take her, and may she make you happier than her mother has made me."

DUCHESS
Sir!

DUKE
If possible. And now there is a little matter to which I think I am entitled to take exception. I come here in state with Her Grace the Duchess and Her Majesty my daughter, and what do I find? Do I find, for instance, a guard of honour to receive me? No!

MARCO and GIULIA
No.

DUKE
The town illuminated? No!

MARCO and GIUSEPPE
No.

DUKE
Refreshment provided? No!

MARCO and GIUSEPPE
No.

DUKE
 A Royal salute fired? No!

MARCO and GIUSEPPE
No.

DUKE
Triumphal arches erected? No!

MARCO and GIUSEPPE
No.

DUKE
The bells set ringing?

MARCO and GIUSEPPE
No.

DUKE
Yes—one—the Visitors', and I rang it myself. It is not enough! It is not enough!

GIUSEPPE
Upon my honour, I'm very sorry; but you see, I was brought up in a gondola, and my ideas of politeness are confined to taking off my cap to my passengers when they tip me.

DUCHESS
That's all very well in its way, but it is not enough.

GIUSEPPE
I'll take off anything else in reason.

DUKE
But a Royal Salute to my daughter—it costs so little.

CASILDA
Papa, I don't want a salute.

GIUSEPPE
My dear sir, as soon as we know which of us is entitled to take that liberty she shall have as many salutes as she likes.

MARCO
As for guards of honour and triumphal arches, you don't know our people—they wouldn't stand it.

GIUSEPPE
They are very off-hand with us—very off-hand indeed.

DUKE
Oh, but you mustn't allow that—you must keep them in proper discipline, you must impress your Court with your importance. You want deportment—carriage—

GIUSEPPE
We've got a carriage.

DUKE
Manner—dignity.
There must be a good deal of this sort of thing—(business)—and a little of this sort of thing—(business)—and possibly just a Soupcon of this sort of thing!—(business)—and so on. Oh, it's very useful, and most effective. Just attend to me. You are a King—I am a subject. Very good—(Gavotte.)

DUKE, DUCHESS, CASILDA, MARCO, GIUSEPPE.

DUKE.
I am a courtier grave and serious
Who is about to kiss your hand:
Try to combine a pose imperious
With a demeanour nobly bland.

MARCO and GIUSEPPE
Let us combine a pose imperious
With a demeanour nobly bland.

(MARCO and GIUSEPPE endeavour to carry out his instructions.)

DUKE
That's, if anything, too unbending—
Too aggressively stiff and grand;

(They suddenly modify their attitudes.)

Now to the other extreme you're tending—
Don't be so deucedly condescending!

DUCHESS and CASILDA
Now to the other extreme you're tending—
Don't be so dreadfully condescending!

MARCO and GIUSEPPE

Oh, hard to please some noblemen seem!
At first, if anything, too unbending;
Off we go to the other extreme—
Too confoundedly condescending!

DUKE
Now a gavotte perform sedately—
Offer your hand with conscious pride;
Take an attitude not too stately,
Still sufficiently dignified.

MARCO and GIUSEPPE
Now for an attitude not too stately,
Still sufficiently dignified.

(They endeavour to carry out his instructions.)

DUKE (beating Oncely, twicely—oncely, twicely—time).
Bow impressively ere you glide.

(They do so.)

Capital both, capital
both—you've caught it nicely!
That is the style of thing precisely!

DUCHESS and CASILDA
Capital both, capital both—they've caught it nicely!
That is the style of thing precisely!

MARCO and GIUSEPPE
Oh, sweet to earn a nobleman's praise!
Capital both, capital both—we've caught it nicely!
Supposing he's right in what he says,
This is the style of thing precisely!

(Gavotte. At the end exeunt DUKE and DUCHESS, leaving CASILDA with MARCO and GIUSEPPE)

GIUSEPPE (to MARCO).
The old birds have gone away and left the young chickens together. That's called tact.

MARCO
It's very awkward. We really ought to tell her how we are situated. It's not fair to the girl.

GIUSEPPE
Then why don't you do it?

MARCO

I'd rather not—you.

GIUSEPPE
I don't know how to begin. (To CASILDA)
Er—Madam—I—we, that is, several of us—

CASILDA
Gentlemen, I am bound to listen to you; but it is right to tell you that, not knowing I was married in infancy, I am over head and ears in love with somebody else.

GIUSEPPE
Our case exactly! We are over head and ears in love with somebody else!

(Enter GIANETTA and TESSA.)

In point of fact, with our wives!

CASILDA
Your wives! Then you are married?

TESSA
It's not our fault.

GIANETTA
We knew nothing about it.

BOTH
We are sisters in misfortune.

CASILDA
My good girls, I don't blame you. Only before we go any further we must really arrive at some satisfactory arrangement, or we shall get hopelessly complicated.

QUINTET AND FINALE.

MARCO, GIUSEPPE, CASILDA, GIANETTA, TESSA

ALL
Here is a case unprecedented!
Here are a King and Queen ill-starred!
Ever since marriage was first invented
Never was known a case so hard!

MARCO
—and I may be said to have been bisected,

GIUSEPPE
By a profound catastrophe!

CASILDA, GIANETTA
Through a calamity unexpected

TESSA
I am divisible into three!

ALL
O moralists all,
How can you call
Marriage a state of unitee,
When excellent husbands are bisected,
And wives divisible into three?
O moralists all,
How can you call
Marriage a state of union true?

CASILDA and GIANETTA,
One-third of myself is married to half of ye

TESSA
—or you,

MARCO and GIUSEPPE
When half of myself has married one-third of ye or you?

(Enter DON ALHAMBRA, followed by DUKE, DUCHESS, and all the CHORUS)

FINALE.

RECITATIVE—**DON ALHAMBRA DEL BOLERO.**
Now let the loyal lieges gather round—
The Prince's foster-mother has been found!
She will declare, to silver clarion's sound,
The rightful King—let him forthwith be crowned!

CHORUS
She will declare, etc.

(DON ALHAMBRA brings forward INEZ, the Prince's foster-mother.)

TESSA
Speak, woman, speak—

DUKE
We're all attention!

GIANETTA

The news we seek-

DUCHESS
This moment mention.

CASILDA
To us they bring—

DON ALHAMBRA DEL BOLERO
His foster-mother.

MARCO
Is he the King?

GIUSEPPE
Or this my brother?

ALL
Speak, woman, speak, etc.

RECITATIVE—**INEZ**.
The Royal Prince was by the King entrusted
To my fond care, ere I grew old and crusted;
When traitors came to steal his son reputed,
My own small boy I deftly substituted!
The villains fell into the trap completely—
I hid the Prince away—still sleeping sweetly:
I called him "son" with pardonable slyness—
His name, Luiz! Behold his Royal Highness!

(Sensation. LUIZ ascends the throne, crowned and robed as King.)

CASILDA (rushing to his arms).
Luiz!

LUIZ
Casilda!

(Embrace.)

ALL
Is this indeed the King?
Oh, wondrous revelation!
Oh, unexpected thing!
Unlooked-for situation!

MARCO, GIANETTA,
This statement we receive

GIUSEPPE, TESSA
With sentiments conflicting;
Our hearts rejoice and grieve,
Each other contradicting;
To those whom we adore
We can be reunited—
On one point rather sore,
But, on the whole, delighted!

LUIZ
When others claimed thy dainty hand,
I waited—waited—waited,

DUKE
As prudence (so I understand)
Dictated—tated—tated.

CASILDA
By virtue of our early vow
Recorded—corded—corded,

DUCHESS
Your pure and patient love is now
Rewarded—warded—warded.

ALL
Then hail, O King of a Golden Land,
And the high-born bride who claims his hand!
The past is dead, and you gain your own,
A royal crown and a golden throne!

(All kneel: LUIZ crowns CASILDA.)

ALL
Once more gondolieri,
Both skilful and wary,
Free from this quandary
Contented are we. Ah!
From Royalty flying,
Our gondolas plying,
And merrily crying
Our "preme," "stali!" Ah!

So good-bye, cachucha, fandango, bolero—
We'll dance a farewell to that measure—
Old Xeres, adieu—Manzanilla—Montero—
We leave you with feelings of pleasure!

CURTAIN

Sir William Schwenck Gilbert was born on November 18th, 1836 at 17 Southampton Street, Strand, London. His father, also named William, was a naval surgeon, who later became a writer of novels and short stories, some of which were illustrated by his son. Gilbert's mother was the former Anne Mary Bye Morris (1812–1888), the daughter of Thomas Morris, an apothecary.

Gilbert's parents were distant and stern, and there was no close bond between either themselves or their children (the marriage was to eventually break up in 1876). Gilbert had three younger sisters, Jane Morris, Anne Maude Mary Florence.

As a child, Gilbert was nicknamed "Bab".

The family travelled to Italy in 1838 and then France before finally returning to settle in London in 1847.

Gilbert was educated in Boulogne, France from age seven, then at Western Grammar School, Brompton, London, before the Great Ealing School, where he became head boy and wrote plays for school performances. He then attended King's College London, graduating in 1856.

His first thought for a career was to take examinations for a commission in the Royal Artillery, but the Crimean War had just ended and with fewer recruits needed only a commission in a line regiment was available. He opted instead for the Civil Service and was an assistant clerk in the Privy Council Office for four years. He hated it. In 1859 he joined the Militia, a part-time volunteer force, and served until 1878, as his other work allowed, and reached the rank of Captain.

To supplement his income Gilbert wrote a variety of stories, comic rants, theatre reviews (many in the form of a parody of the play being reviewed), and, using the pseudonym of his childhood nickname, "Bab" illustrated poems for several comic magazines, primarily Fun, started in 1861. His work was also published in the Cornhill Magazine, London Society, Tinsley's Magazine and Temple Bar. Gilbert was also the London correspondent for L'Invalide Russe and a drama critic for the Illustrated London Times. In the 1860s he also contributed to Tom Hood's Christmas annuals, to Saturday Night, the Comic News and the Savage Club Papers.

The poems, illustrated humorously by Gilbert, proved immensely popular and were reprinted in book form as the Bab Ballads. He would later return to many of these as source material for his plays and comic operas.

In 1863 he received a bequest of £300 allowing him to leave the civil service and attempt a career as a barrister. Unfortunately, he managed to attract few clients.

However, these events happily coincided with his first professionally produced play; Uncle Baby, which ran for seven weeks in the autumn of 1863.

In 1865–66, Gilbert collaborated with Charles Millward on several pantomimes, including Hush-a-Bye, Baby, On the Tree Top, or, Harlequin Fortunia, King Frog of Frog Island, and the Magic Toys of Lowther Arcade (1866).

Gilbert's first solo success, however, came a few days after Hush-a-Bye Baby premiered. His friend and mentor, Tom Robertson, was asked to deliver a pantomime within two weeks. Robertson couldn't and recommended Gilbert who took the job. Written and rushed to the stage in 10 days, Dulcamara, or the Little Duck and the Great Quack, a burlesque of Gaetano Donizetti's L'elisir d'amore, proved very popular. This led to a long series of further Gilbert opera burlesques, pantomimes and farces, full of dreadful puns, but showing signs of the satire that would later be such an integral part of Gilbert's work.

After a failed relationship with the novelist Annie Thomas, Gilbert married Lucy Agnes Turner, whom he affectionately called "Kitty", in 1867; she was 11 years his junior. They were socially active both in London and later at their new home at Grim's Dyke, often holding dinner parties. Although they had no children they had many pets, including several exotic ones.

Next followed Gilbert's biggest success so far; his penultimate operatic parody, Robert the Devil, a burlesque of Giacomo Meyerbeer's opera, Robert le diable, part of a triple bill that opened the Gaiety Theatre, London in 1868. It ran for over 100 nights.

In Victorian theatre, Gilbert's burlesques were considered very tasteful compared to the offerings of others. He would now move away from burlesque to plays with original plots and fewer puns. His first was An Old Score in 1869.

Theatre, at this time had fallen into disrepute. London was awash with poorly translated French operettas and cheaply written, prurient Victorian burlesques. From 1869 to 1875, Gilbert joined with Thomas German Reed (and his wife Priscilla), whose Gallery of Illustration sought to regain some of theatre's lost respect with family entertainments. This would be so successful that by 1885 Gilbert could safely state that original British plays were appropriate for an innocent 15-year-old girl to watch.

The initial work for the Gallery of Illustration, No Cards, was the first of six musical entertainments for the German Reeds, by Gilbert some with music composed by Thomas German Reed.

The German Reeds' intimate theatre allowed Gilbert to develop a personal style that would also cede to him control all aspects of production; set, costumes, direction and stage management.

Gilbert's first big hit at the Gallery of Illustration, Ages Ago, also opened in 1869. It marked the beginning of a collaboration with the composer Frederic Clay that would last seven years and cover four works. It was at a rehearsal for Ages Ago that Clay introduced Gilbert to Arthur Sullivan.

These musical works gave Gilbert a valuable education as a lyricist and he perfected the 'topsy-turvy' style that he had been developing in his Bab Ballads, where the humour was derived by setting up a ridiculous premise and following through on its logical consequences, however absurd they might be.

Ever busy he found time to create several 'fairy comedies' at the Haymarket Theatre. The premise was the idea of self-revelation by characters under the influence of magic or some supernatural experience. The first was The Palace of Truth (1870), based partly on a story by Madame de Genlis. In 1871, with Pygmalion and Galatea, one of seven plays that he produced that year, Gilbert scored his greatest hit to date. Together, these plays including The Wicked World (1873), Sweethearts (1874), and Broken Hearts (1875), did for Gilbert on the dramatic stage what the German Reed entertainments had done for him on the musical stage: they established that his talents were large and burgeoning, a writer of wide range, as comfortable with human drama as much as farcical humour.

Contemptorous with this period Gilbert pushed the satirical boundaries. He collaborated with Gilbert Arthur à Beckett on The Happy Land (1873), in part, a parody of his own The Wicked World, which was briefly banned because of its caricatures of Gladstone and his ministers. Similarly, The Realm of Joy (1873) was set in the lobby of a theatre performing a scandalous play (implied to be the Happy Land), with many jokes at the expense of the Lord Chamberlain (the "Lord High Disinfectant", as he's referred to in the play). In Charity (1874), however, Gilbert uses the freedom of the stage in a different way: to illuminate the contrasting ways in which society treated men and women who had sex outside of marriage. It was ground breaking and some see it as anticipating the 'problem plays' of Shaw and Ibsen.

Once established as a writer Gilbert was also the stage director, with strong, forceful opinions on how they should best be performed.

In Gilbert's 1874 burlesque, Rosencrantz and Guildenstern, the character Hamlet, in his speech to the players, sums up Gilbert's theory of comic acting: "I hold that there is no such antick fellow as your bombastical hero who doth so earnestly spout forth his folly as to make his hearers believe that he is unconscious of all incongruity". Again some say with this he prepared the ground for playwrights such as George Bernard Shaw and Oscar Wilde to be able to flourish.

Tom Robertson had "introduced Gilbert both to the revolutionary notion of disciplined rehearsals and to mise-en-scène or unity of style in the whole presentation – direction, design, music, acting." Like Robertson, Gilbert demanded discipline in his actors, that they know their lines, enunciate them clearly and keep to his stage directions, a new development for actors at the time. It also ushered in the replacement of the star with the disciplined ensemble.

Gilbert was meticulous in his preparations, making models of the stage and designing every action in advance. He refused to work with actors who challenged him. He was famous for demonstrating the action himself, even as he grew older. Such was his interest in standards that even during long runs and revivals, he closely supervised the performances of his plays, making sure that no one made additions or deletions.

Arthur Sullivan – A Short Biography

Sir Arthur Seymour Sullivan, MVO was born on May 13th 1842 in Lambeth, London. His father, Thomas Sullivan, a military bandmaster, clarinetist and music teacher, was born in Ireland and raised in Chelsea, London, and his mother, Mary Clementina (née Coghlan, English born, of Irish and Italian descent. Thomas Sullivan was based from 1845 to 1857 at the Royal Military College, Sandhurst, where he was the bandmaster and taught music privately to supplement his income. Young Sullivan became proficient with many of the instruments in the band and had composed an anthem, "By the waters of Babylon", by the age of eight. While proudly observing his son's obvious musical talent, he knew, at first hand, how insecure a profession it was and discouraged him from pursuing it.

Three years later whilst at a private school in Bayswater, Sullivan persuaded his parents and headmaster to allow him to apply for membership in the choir of the Chapel Royal. There were concerns that Sullivan at nearly 12 years of age was too old to be a treble as his voice would soon break. But he was accepted and soon became a soloist and, by 1856, was promoted to "first boy". Troublingly, even at this age, Sullivan's health was delicate, and he was easily fatigued.

However, Sullivan flourished under the training of the Reverend Thomas Helmore, and began to compose anthems and songs. Helmore arranged for one pieces, "O Israel", to be published in 1855.

In 1856, the Royal Academy of Music awarded the first Mendelssohn Scholarship to the 14-year-old Sullivan, granting him a year's training at the academy. His principal teacher there was John Goss, whose own teacher had been a pupil of Mozart. Initially Sullivan studied piano.

Sullivan's scholarship was extended to a second year, and then a third so that he could study in Germany, at the Leipzig Conservatoire. There he was trained in Mendelssohn's ideas and techniques as well as being exposed to Schubert, Verdi, Bach, and Wagner. Sullivan was an eager pupil and always looking for inspiration. On a visit to a synagogue, he was so struck by some of the cadences and progressions in the music that three decades later he would recall them for use in his serious opera, Ivanhoe.

Though the scholarship in Leipzig, was for one year he stayed for three. Sullivan credited his Leipzig period with rapid and sustained musical growth. His graduation piece, in 1861, was a set of incidental music to Shakespeare's The Tempest. Revised and expanded, it was performed at the Crystal Palace in 1862, a year after his return to London. It was an immediate sensation. He began building a reputation as England's most promising young composer.

He now embarked on composing with a series of ambitious works, interspersed with hymns, parlour songs and other light pieces of a more commercial nature. These compositions could not support him financially, and from 1861 to 1872 he supplemented his income working as a church organist, a task he enjoyed, and as a music teacher, sometimes at the Crystal Palace School, which he hated and gave up as soon as his finances allowed. Sullivan also took an early chance to compose pieces for royalty with the wedding of the Prince of Wales in 1863.

Sullivan began to put voice and orchestra together with The Masque at Kenilworth (Birmingham Festival, 1864). For Covent Garden that same year he composed his first ballet, L'Île Enchantée.

1865 saw Sullivan initiated into Freemasonry and was Grand Organist of the United Grand Lodge of England in 1887 during Queen Victoria's Golden Jubilee.

In 1866, he premiered his Irish Symphony and Cello Concerto, his only works in these genres. In the same year, his Overture in C (In Memoriam), commemorating the recent death of his father, was a commission from the Norwich Festival.

His overture Marmion was premiered by the Philharmonic Society in 1867. The Times called it "another step in advance on the part of the only composer of any remarkable promise that just at present we can boast."

Sadly, his initial attempt at opera, The Sapphire Necklace (1863–64) with a libretto by Henry F. Chorley, was not produced and, apart from the Overture and two songs published separately, is now lost.

His first surviving opera, Cox and Box (1866), was written for a private performance. It then received charity performances in London and Manchester, and was later produced at the Gallery of Illustration, where it ran for an extraordinary 264 performances. His soon to be partner, W. S. Gilbert, writing in Fun magazine, announced the score as superior to F. C. Burnand's libretto.

In 1867 Sullivan and Burnand were commissioned by Thomas German Reed for a two-act opera, The Contrabandista (revised and expanded as The Chieftain in 1894), but it was a much more modest success.

Sullivan wrote a group of seven part songs in 1868, the best-known of which is "The Long Day Closes". His last major work of the 1860s was a short oratorio, The Prodigal Son, which premiered in Worcester Cathedral as part of the 1869 Three Choirs Festival to much praise.

The Overture di Ballo, Sullivan's most enduring work, was composed for the Birmingham Festival in 1870.

1871 was a busy year. Sullivan published his only song cycle, The Window; or, The Songs of the Wrens, to words by Tennyson, and wrote the first of a series of suites of incidental music for West End productions of Shakespeare plays. Later in the year he composed a dramatic cantata, On Shore and Sea, for the opening of the London International Exhibition, and the beautiful hymn Onward, Christian Soldiers, with words by Sabine Baring-Gould. The Salvation Army adopted it and it has become one of Britain's best loved hymns.

Gilbert & Sullivan – The Collaboration Begins

In 1871, John Hollingshead commissioned Gilbert to work with Sullivan on a holiday piece for Christmas, entitled Thespis, or The Gods Grown Old, at the Gaiety Theatre. It was a success and its run was extended beyond the length of the Gaiety's normal run. And that seemed to be that.

Gilbert and Sullivan now went their separate ways. Gilbert worked again with Clay on Happy Arcadia (1872), and with Alfred Cellier on Topsyturveydom (1874), as well as several farces, operetta libretti, extravaganzas, fairy comedies, adaptations from novels, translations from the French. In 1874, he published his last piece for Fun magazine ("Rosencrantz and Guildenstern"), almost three years after his last and then promptly resigned citing disapproval of the new owner's other publishing interests.

Sullivan was busy on large-scale works in the early 1870s with the Festival Te Deum (Crystal Palace, 1872); and the oratorio, The Light of the World (Birmingham Festival, 1873). He also wrote suites of incidental music for productions of The Merry Wives of Windsor at the Gaiety in 1874 and Henry VIII at the Theatre Royal, Manchester in 1877 as well as continuing composing hymns.

In 1873, Sullivan had also contributed songs to Burnand's Christmas "drawing room extravaganza", The Miller and His Man.

By 1875 conditions were right for Gilbert and Sullivan to work together again. Back in 1868, Gilbert had published a short comedic libretto in Fun magazine entitled "Trial by Jury: An Operetta". In 1873, Gilbert had arranged with theatrical manager and composer, Carl Rosa, to expand this work into a one-act libretto. It was arranged that Rosa's wife was to sing the role of the plaintiff. Tragically, Rosa's wife died in childbirth in 1874. Gilbert offered the libretto to Richard D'Oyly Carte, but Carte could not use the piece at that time.

The project seemed grounded. A few months later Carte, was managing the Royalty Theatre, needed a short piece to pair with Offenbach's La Périchole. Carte had previously conducted Sullivan's Cox and Box and remembering that Gilbert had suggested a libretto to him, he reunited Gilbert and Sullivan. The result was the one-act comic opera Trial by Jury. Starring Sullivan's brother Fred as the Learned Judge, it became a surprise hit, as well as earning lavish praise from the critics. It played for over 300 performances in its first few seasons.

A short time after Trial had opened Sullivan wrote The Zoo, another one-act comic opera, with a libretto by B. C. Stephenson. It did not perform well. Now the path was clear for Gilbert & Sullivan to reteam together in earnest and dominate light opera for the next 15 years.

Light opera was not considered of much worth by serious critics. Gilbert wanted greater respect for himself and his profession. At that time plays were not published in a form suitable for a "gentleman's library", they were in the main cheap and unattractive in their look designed mainly for use by actors rather than the home reader. Gilbert now arranged in late 1875 for the publishers Chatto and Windus to print a volume of his plays in a format designed to appeal to the general reader, with an attractive binding and clear type, containing Gilbert's most respectable plays, including his most serious works, and mischievously capped off with Trial by Jury.

After the success of Trial by Jury, there were discussions towards reviving Thespis, but Gilbert and Sullivan were not able to agree on terms with Carte and his backers. The score to Thespis was never published, and tragically most of the music is now lost.

Carte took some time to gather together funds for another opera, and in this gap the ever-busy Gilbert produced several works including Tom Cobb (1875), Eyes and No Eyes (1875), and Princess Toto (1876), his last and most ambitious work with Clay, a three-act comic opera with full orchestra. He also found time to write two serious works, Broken Hearts (1875) and Dan'l Druce, Blacksmith (1876) and his most successful comic play, Engaged (1877), which inspired Oscar Wilde's The Importance of Being Earnest.

It was only by 1877 that Carte finally assembled enough investors to form the Comedy Opera Company with a mandate to launch a series of original English comic operas, beginning with a third collaboration between Gilbert and Sullivan, The Sorcerer, in November 1877.

The Sorcerer (1877), ran for 178 performances, a success by the standards of the day, but H.M.S. Pinafore (1878), which followed it, turned Gilbert and Sullivan into an international phenomenon. The bright and cheerful music of Pinafore was composed during a time when Sullivan was in the middle of a health scare. He was in terrible pain from a kidney stone. H.M.S. Pinafore ran for 571 performances in London, the then-second-longest theatrical run in history, it also gave birth to and more than 150 unauthorised productions in America alone. Although this increased the reach of their reputations it added nothing to their profits.

It was noted in the Times review of H.M.S. Pinafore that the opera was an early attempt at the establishment of a "national musical stage" ... free from risqué French "improprieties" and without the "aid" of Italian and German musical models.

As the profits rolled in came acrimony among the investors who felt the shares were unequal. One night the other Comedy Opera Company partners hired thugs to storm the theatre to steal the sets and costumes in order that they could mount a rival production. This was beaten off by stagehands and others at the theatre loyal to Carte. Carte was to now continue as sole impresario of the newly renamed D'Oyly Carte Opera Company.

For the next decade, the Savoy Operas were Gilbert's principal activity. The successful comic operas with Sullivan continued to appear every year or two, several of them being among the longest-running productions of the musical stage. After Pinafore came The Pirates of Penzance (1879), Patience (1881), Iolanthe (1882), Princess Ida (1884 and based on Gilbert's earlier farce, The Princess), The Mikado (1885), Ruddigore (1887), The Yeomen of the Guard (1888), and The Gondoliers (1889). Gilbert not only directed and oversaw all aspects of production, but he designed the costumes himself for Patience, Iolanthe, Princess Ida, and Ruddigore. He insisted on precise and authentic sets and costumes, which provided a foundation to ground and focus his absurd characters and situations.

In 1878, Gilbert realised a lifelong dream to play Harlequin, which he did at the Gaiety Theatre in an amateur charity production of The Forty Thieves, written partly by himself. Gilbert trained for Harlequin's stylised dancing with his friend John D'Auban, who had arranged the dances for some of his plays and would choreograph most of the Gilbert and Sullivan operas. Producer John Hollingshead later remembered, "the gem of the performance was the grimly earnest and determined Harlequin of W. S. Gilbert. It gave me an idea of what Oliver Cromwell would have made of the character."

In 1879, Sullivan suggested to a reporter from The New York Times the secret of his success with Gilbert: "His ideas are as suggestive for music as they are quaint and laughable. His numbers ... always give me musical ideas."

During this time, Gilbert and Sullivan also collaborated on one other major work. In 1880, Sullivan was appointed director of the triennial Leeds Music Festival. For his first festival he was commissioned to write a sacred choral work. He chose Henry Hart Milman's 1822 dramatic poem based on the life and death of Saint Margaret the Virgin for its basis. It premiered at the Leeds music festival in October 1880. Gilbert arranged the original epic poem by Henry Hart Milman into a libretto suitable for the music.

Carte opened the next Gilbert and Sullivan piece, Patience, in April 1881 at London's Opera Comique, where their past three operas had played. In October, Patience transferred to the new, larger, state-of-the-art (it was the first theatre to be lit entirely with electricity) Savoy Theatre, built with the profits of the previous Gilbert and Sullivan works.

From now on all of the partnership's collaborations were produced at the Savoy. The first to actually premiere here was Iolanthe in 1882, it was their fourth hit in a row.

Cracks were beginning to surface between the partners. Sullivan, despite the financial security, began to view his work with Gilbert as beneath his skills, as well as being repetitious. After Iolanthe, Sullivan had not intended to write a new work with Gilbert, but when his broker went bankrupt in late 1882 he suffered serious financial loss. Needs must and Sullivan buckled down to continue writing Savoy operas.

In February 1883, he and Gilbert signed a five-year agreement with Carte, requiring them to produce a new comic opera on six months' notice.

The ever watchful Gilbert had the previous year installed a telephone in his home and another at the prompt desk at the Savoy Theatre, so that he could listen in on performances and rehearsals from his home study. Gilbert had referred to the new technology in Pinafore in 1878, only two years after the device was invented and before London even had telephones.

Better news arrived for Sullivan on May 22nd, 1883, when he was knighted by Queen Victoria for his "services ... rendered to the promotion of the art of music" in Britain. The musical establishment, and many critics, believed that this would put an end to his career as a composer of comic opera – that a musical knight should not stoop below oratorio or grand opera. But Sullivan having just signed the five-year agreement and the financial security that gave him could no nothing to change course now.

The next opera, Princess Ida in 1884, which was the duo's only three-act, blank verse work, stuttered. Its run was much shorter. Sullivan's score was praised but with box office receipts lagging in March 1884, Carte gave the six months' notice, under the partnership contract, requiring a new opera.

Sullivan's friend, composer Frederic Clay, had suffered a serious stroke in early December 1883 that ended his career at only 45 years of age. Sullivan, with his own longstanding kidney problems, and his desire to devote himself to more serious music, replied to Carte, "It is impossible for me to do another piece of the character of those already written by Gilbert and myself."

Gilbert however was already at work on it. His idea revolved around a plot in which people fell in love against their wills after taking a magic lozenge. Sullivan was unequoviacal in his response. On April 1st, 1884 he wrote that he had "come to the end of my tether with the operas. I have been continually keeping down the music in order that not one syllable should be lost.... I should like to set a story of human interest & probability where the humorous words would come in a humorous not serious situation, & where, if the situation were a tender or dramatic one the words would be of similar character."

There was now a lengthy exchange of correspondence in which Sullivan called Gilbert's plot sketch (particularly the "lozenge" element) unacceptably mechanical, and too similar in both its grotesque "elements of topsyturveydom" and in actual plot to their earlier work, especially The Sorcerer, and requested, time and again, that a new subject be found.

This impasse was finally resolved on May 8th when Gilbert proposed a plot that would be their most successful: The Mikado (1885). It was to run for a staggering 672 performances.

In 1886, Sullivan composed his last large-scale choral work of the decade. It was a cantata for the Leeds Festival, The Golden Legend, based on Longfellow's poem of the same name. Apart from the comic operas, this proved to be Sullivan's best received full-length work. It was given hundreds of performances during his lifetime alone.

Ruddigore followed The Mikado in 1887. It was profitable, but its nine-month run was deemed to be disappointing compared with the earlier Savoy operas.

Gilbert was always keen to use a good idea again and proposed for their next piece another version of the magic lozenge plot. It was immediately rejected by Sullivan. Gilbert finally proposed a quite serious opera, to which Sullivan was in agreement. Although not a grand opera, The Yeomen of the Guard (1888) gave him the opportunity to compose his most ambitious stage work to date. In 1885, Sullivan had told an interviewer, ""The opera of the future is a compromise (among the French, German and Italian schools) – a sort of eclectic school, a selection of the merits of each one. I myself will make an attempt to produce a grand opera of this new school. ... Yes, it will be an historical work, and it is the dream of my life."

After The Yeomen of the Guard opened, Sullivan turned once again to Shakespeare and composed incidental music for Henry Irving's production of Macbeth (1888).

Sullivan wished to produce further serious works with Gilbert. He had collaborated with no other librettist since 1875. Gilbert felt the reaction to The Yeomen of the Guard had "not been so convincing as to warrant us in assuming that the public want something more earnest still." Gilbert countered by proposing that Sullivan should go ahead with his plan to write a grand opera, as well as comic works for the Savoy. Sullivan was not immediately persuaded. He replied, "I have lost the liking for writing comic opera, and entertain very grave doubts as to my power of doing it."

Nevertheless, Sullivan soon commissioned a grand opera libretto from Julian Sturgis (the recommendation came from Gilbert), while suggesting to Gilbert that he revive an old idea for an opera set in colourful Venice. The comic opera was completed first in 1889. The Gondoliers has been described as a pinnacle of Sullivan's achievement. It was to be the last great Gilbert and Sullivan success.

In April 1890, during the run of The Gondoliers, Gilbert objected to Carte's financial accounts which included a charge to the partnership for the cost of new carpeting for the Savoy Theatre lobby. Gilbert believed that this was a maintenance expense that should be charged to Carte alone. Carte who was building a new theatre to present Sullivan's forthcoming grand opera was adamant that it was legitimate. Sullivan sided with Carte, even going so far as to testify erroneously as to certain old debts.

The partners were in fundamental disagreement and the relationship was for all intents and purposes ruptured.

Gilbert took legal action against Carte and Sullivan and refused to write a word more for the Savoy. Sullivan wrote to Gilbert in September 1890 that he was "physically and mentally ill over this wretched business. I have not yet got over the shock of seeing our names coupled ... in hostile antagonism over a few miserable pounds".

From Gilbert's point of view Carte had either made a series of serious blunders in the accounts, or deliberately attempted to swindle his partners.

Gilbert wrote to Sullivan on May 28th, 1891, a year after the end of the "Quarrel", that Carte had admitted "an unintentional overcharge of nearly £1,000 in the electric lighting accounts alone." It seemed to illustrate Gilbert's point.

Work beckoned for Gilbert and he got on with it. He wrote The Mountebanks with Alfred Cellier and then a flop Haste to the Wedding with George Grossmith. Sullivan wrote Haddon Hall with Sydney Grundy.

In the Courts Gilbert prevailed in the lawsuit and felt vindicated. Although there was acrimony and bitterness between them the partnership had been so profitable that, after the financial failure of the Royal English Opera House, Carte and his wife sought to reunite the author and composer.

In 1891, after numerous failed attempts at a reconciliation, Tom Chappell, the music publisher who printed the Gilbert and Sullivan operas, stepped in to mediate between his two most profitable artists, and within two weeks, against the odds, had succeeded. The result was to be two more operas: Utopia, Limited (1893) and The Grand Duke (1896).

A third was almost achieved when Gilbert offered a third libretto to Sullivan (His Excellency, 1894), but his insistence on casting Nancy McIntosh, his protegée from Utopia, led to Sullivan's refusal.

Utopia, was only a modest success, and The Grand Duke, in which a theatrical troupe, by means of a "statutory duel" and a conspiracy, takes political control of a grand duchy, was a failure.

The partnership now ended for good.

Graciously Gilbert would late write, "... Savoy opera was snuffed out by the deplorable death of my distinguished collaborator, Sir Arthur Sullivan. When that event occurred, I saw no one with whom I felt that I could work with satisfaction and success, and so I discontinued to write libretti."

WS Gilbert – Life After the Partnership

In 1889 Gilbert financed the building of the Garrick Theatre. The following year the Gilberts moved to Grim's Dyke in Harrow. In 1891, Gilbert was appointed Justice of the Peace for Middlesex. After casting Nancy McIntosh in Utopia, Limited, he and Lady Gilbert developed an affection for her, and she eventually gained the status of an unofficially adopted daughter, moving to Grim's Dyke to live with them. She continued living there, even after Gilbert's death, until Lady Gilbert's death in 1936.

Although Gilbert announced a retirement from the theatre after the poor initial run of his last work with Sullivan, The Grand Duke (1896) and the poor reception of his 1897 play The Fortune Hunter, he produced at least three more plays over the last dozen years of his life, including an unsuccessful opera, Fallen Fairies (1909), with Edward German.

Gilbert, as we know was very keen on keeping his plays in the shape they were originally intended and continued to supervise the various revivals of his works by the D'Oyly Carte Opera Company, including its London Repertory seasons in 1906–09.

The last play he wrote, The Hooligan, produced just four months before his death, is a study of a young condemned thug in a prison cell. Gilbert shows sympathy for his protagonist, the son of a thief who, brought up among thieves, kills his girlfriend.

This grim, yet powerful piece, became one of Gilbert's most successful serious dramas, and it is easy to see why many thought he was developing a new style only for death to rob of us of what would surely be a fascinating journey.

In these last years, Gilbert wrote children's book versions of H.M.S. Pinafore and The Mikado giving, in some cases, backstory that is not found in the librettos.

Official recognition for him came on July 15th, 1907 with his knighthood in recognition of his contributions to drama. Gilbert was the first British writer ever to receive a knighthood for his plays alone—earlier dramatist knights were knighted for political and other services.

On May 29th, 1911, Gilbert was about to give a swimming lesson to Winifred Isabel Emery and 17-year-old Ruby Preece in the lake of his home, Grim's Dyke, when Preece lost her footing and called for help. Gilbert dived in to save her but suffered a heart attack in the middle of the lake and died.

William Schwenck was cremated at Golders Green and his ashes buried at the Church of St. John the Evangelist, Stanmore. The inscription on Gilbert's memorial on the south wall of the Thames Embankment in London reads: "His Foe was Folly, and his Weapon Wit".

George Grossmith wrote to The Daily Telegraph that, although Gilbert had been described as an autocrat at rehearsals, "That was really only his manner when he was playing the part of stage director at rehearsals. As a matter of fact, he was a generous, kind true gentleman, and I use the word in the purest and original sense."

Gilbert's legacy, aside from building the Garrick Theatre are the canon of Savoy Operas and other works that are either still being performed or in print all these years later. He has made a lasting and defining influence on both the American and British musical theatre. The innovations in content and form of the works that he and Sullivan developed, and in Gilbert's theories of acting and stage direction, directly influenced the development of the modern musical throughout the 20th century. Gilbert's lyrics use punning, as well as complex internal and two and three-syllable rhyme schemes, and served as a model for such 20th century Broadway lyricists as P.G. Wodehouse, Cole Porter, Ira Gershwin, and Lorenz Hart.

Gilbert's influence on the English language has also been marked, with well-known phrases such as "A policeman's lot is not a happy one", "short, sharp shock", "What never? Well, hardly ever!", and "let the punishment fit the crime" arising from his pen.

Arthur Sullivan – Life After the Partnership

Sullivan's only grand opera, Ivanhoe, based on Walter Scott's novel, opened at Carte's new Royal English Opera House on January 31st, 1891. Sullivan completed the score too late to meet Carte's planned production date, and costs had overrun to such an extent that Carte insisted on a contractual penalty of £3,000 for the delay. However, when it opened it ran 155 consecutive performances, a wonderful run for a serious opera, and garnered good reviews. Afterwards, Carte was unable to fill the new opera house with other productions, and, unfairly, Ivanhoe was blamed for the failure of the opera house.

Later in 1891, New York beckoned for Sullivan and his music for Tennyson's The Foresters, which ran at Daly's Theatre in New York in 1892, but failed in London the following year.

Sullivan returned to comic opera, but needed a new collaborator. His next piece was Haddon Hall in 1892, with a libretto by Sydney Grundy based somewhat loosely on the elopement of Dorothy Vernon with John Manners. Although still comic, the tone and style of the work was more serious and romantic than the operas with Gilbert. It nonetheless enjoyed a run of 204 performances, and earned critical praise.

In 1894 Sullivan teamed up again with F. C. Burnand for The Chieftain, a heavily-reworked version of their earlier two-act opera, The Contrabandista, alas it failed.

The following year Sullivan provided incidental music for the Lyceum, this time for J. Comyns Carr's King Arthur.

As we know Gilbert and Sullivan did reunite for The Grand Duke in 1896. But it failed and they never worked together again. This did not affect the constant revival of their earlier operas at the Savoy.

In May 1897, Sullivan's full-length ballet, Victoria and Merrie England, opened at the Alhambra Theatre in celebration of the Queen's Diamond Jubilee. The work's seven scenes celebrate English history and culture, with the Victorian period as the grand finale. It ran for six months which was a great achievement. Following this was The Beauty Stone in 1898, with a libretto by Arthur Wing Pinero and J. Comyns Carr. Based on mediaeval morality plays the opera was a critical failure and, on the whole, a commercial failure running for only seven weeks.

Success came in 1899, to benefit "the wives and children of soldiers and sailors" on active service in the Boer War, when Sullivan composed the music of a jingoistic song, "The Absent-Minded Beggar", to a text by Rudyard Kipling. It was a sensation and raised a staggering £250,000 from performances and the sale of sheet music and other merchandise. Later that year he returned to his comic roots with In The Rose of Persia, with a libretto by Basil Hood overlapping a setting of exotic Arabian Nights with plot elements of The Mikado. It was well received, and, apart from those with Gilbert, was his most successful full-length collaboration. Another opera with Hood, The Emerald Isle, quickly went into preparation, but sadly Sullivan died before it completion.

On November 22nd, 1900 Arthur Seymour Sullivan died of heart failure, following an attack of bronchitis, at his flat in London. The unfinished opera, The Emerald Isle, was completed by Edward German and premiered in 1901. His Te Deum Laudamus, written to commemorate the end of the Boer War, was performed posthumously.

Sullivan wished to be buried in Brompton Cemetery with his parents and brother, but by order of the Queen he was buried in St. Paul's Cathedral. In addition to his knighthood, honours awarded to Sullivan in his lifetime included Doctor in Music, honoris causa, by the universities of Cambridge (1876) and Oxford (1879); Chevalier, Légion d'honneur, France (1878); The Order of the Medjidieh conferred by the Sultan of Turkey (1888); and appointment as a Member of the Fourth Class of the Royal Victorian Order (MVO) in 1897.

In all, Sullivan's artistic output included 23 operas, 13 major orchestral works, eight choral works and oratorios, two ballets, one song cycle, incidental music to several plays, numerous hymns and other church pieces, and a large body of songs, parlour ballads, part songs, carols, and piano and chamber pieces.

Although Sullivan had several long term affairs and was also known to have a roving eye that led him to frequent liaisons with many other women he never married.

Rachel Scott Russell was the first of his great loves. Her parents' disapproval meant they met secretly but by 1868, Sullivan was enmeshed in a simultaneous and secret affair with Rachel's sister Louise. Both relationships had ceased by early 1869.

Sullivan's affair with the American socialite, Fanny Ronalds, a woman three years his senior, who had two children began when they met in Paris around 1867. The affair began in earnest soon after she moved to London in 1871. Despite his wandering ways she was a constant companion up to the time of Sullivan's death, but around 1889 or 1890, the sexual relationship seems to have ended.

In 1896, the 54-year-old Sullivan proposed marriage to 22-year-old Violet Beddington but she refused.

The favourite playgrounds for Sullivan were Paris and the south of France, with friends ranging from European royalty to Claude Debussy, and where the casinos enabled him to indulge his passion for gambling.

Sullivan enjoyed playing tennis although, according to George Grossmith, "I have seen some bad lawn-tennis players in my time, but I never saw anyone so bad as Arthur Sullivan".

He was devoted to his parents, particularly his mother, until her death in 1882. Henry Lytton wrote, "I believe there was never a more affectionate tie than that which existed between Sullivan and his mother, a very witty old lady, and one who took an exceptional pride in her son's accomplishments.

Sullivan once explained his method of working; "I don't use the piano in composition – that would limit me terribly". Sullivan explained that he did not wait for inspiration, but had "to dig for it. ... I decide on the rhythm before I come to the question of melody. ... I mark out the metre in dots and dashes, and not until I have quite settled on the rhythm do I proceed to actual notation."

In composing the Savoy operas, Sullivan wrote the vocal lines of the musical numbers first, and these were given to the actors. He, or an assistant, improvised a piano accompaniment at the early rehearsals; he wrote the orchestrations later, after he had seen what Gilbert's stage business would be. He left the overtures until last and often delegated their composition, based on his outlines, to his assistants, often adding his suggestions or corrections. Those Sullivan wrote himself include Thespis, Iolanthe, Princess Ida, The Yeomen of the Guard, The Gondoliers, The Grand Duke and probably Utopia Limited. Most of the overtures are structured as a potpourri of tunes from the operas in three sections: fast, slow and fast. The overtures from the Gilbert and Sullivan operas remain popular. Sullivan invariably conducted the operas on their opening nights.

In general, Sullivan preferred to write in major keys. In the Savoy operas less than 5% of the numbers are in a minor key and even in his serious works the major prevails. Sullivan was happy on occasion to use chords traditionally considered technically incorrect. When reproached for using consecutive fifths in Cox and Box, he replied "if 5ths turn up it doesn't matter, so long as there is no offence to the ear."

Sullivan's orchestra for the Savoy Operas was typical of any other pit orchestra of his era: 2 flutes (+ piccolo), oboe, 2 clarinets, bassoon, 2 horns, 2 cornets, 2 trombones, timpani, percussion and strings. According to Geoffrey Toye, the number of players in the Savoy orchestra was originally 31. Sullivan argued hard for an increase in the pit orchestra's size, and starting with The Yeomen of the Guard, the orchestra was augmented with a second bassoon and a bass trombone. Sullivan generally orchestrated each score at almost the last moment, noting that the accompaniment for an opera had to wait until he saw the staging, so that he could judge how heavily or lightly to orchestrate each part of the music. For his large-scale orchestral pieces, Sullivan added a second oboe part, sometimes double bassoon and bass clarinet, more horns, trumpets, tuba, and sometimes an organ and/or a harp. Many of these pieces used very large orchestras.

Sullivan's critical reputation has undergone extreme changes since he first came to prominence in the 1860s. At first, critics were struck by his potential, and he was hailed as the long-awaited great English composer. His incidental music to The Tempest received an acclaimed premiere at the Crystal Palace just before Sullivan's 20th birthday in April 1862. The Athenaeum wrote:

When Sullivan turned to comic opera with Gilbert, the serious critics began to express disapproval. Peter Gammond writes of "misapprehensions and prejudices, delivered to our door by the Victorian firm Musical Snobs Ltd. ... frivolity and high spirits were sincerely seen as elements that could not be exhibited by anyone who was to be admitted to the sanctified society of Art." As early as 1877 The Figaro wrote that Sullivan "has all the ability to make him a great composer, but he wilfully throws his opportunity away. ... He possesses all the natural ability to have given us an English opera, and, instead, he affords us a little more-or-less excellent fooling." Few critics denied the excellence of Sullivan's theatre scores. The Theatre wrote that "Iolanthe sustains Dr Sullivan's reputation as the most spontaneous, fertile, and scholarly composer of comic opera this country has ever produced." However, comic opera, no matter how skilfully crafted, was viewed as an intrinsically lower form of art than oratorio. The Athenaeum's review of The Martyr of Antioch declared: "It is an advantage to have the composer of H.M.S. Pinafore occupying himself with a worthier form of art."

Although the more solemn members of the musical establishment could not forgive Sullivan for writing music that was both comic and accessible, he was, nevertheless, "the nation's de facto composer laureate".

Gilbert & Sullivan – A Concise Bibliography

The Collaborative Pieces

All of these operas are full-length two-act works, except for Trial by Jury, which is in one act, and Princess Ida, which is three acts.

Thespis (1871)
Trial by Jury (1875)
The Sorcerer (1877)
H.M.S. Pinafore (1878)
The Pirates of Penzance (1879)
Patience (1881)
Iolanthe (1882)
Princess Ida (1884)
The Mikado (1885)

Ruddigore (1887)
The Yeomen of the Guard (1888)
The Gondoliers (1889)
Utopia, Limited (1893)
The Grand Duke (1896)

W.S. Gilbert – his Other Works

Poetry
The Bab Ballads, a collection of comic verse published roughly between 1865 and 1871
Songs of a Savoyard, London, 1890, a collection of Gilbert's song lyrics.

Short Stories
Foggerty's Fairy & Other Tales, a collection of short stories and essays, mainly from before 1874.

Some other short stories but not in the above appear here:-

Belgravia, Vol. 2 (1867). "From St. Paul's to Piccadilly," pp. 67–74
Fun, Vol. 1 new series (1865-1866) (several contributions by Gilbert; near end of volume)
Fun Christmas Number 1865, ("The Astounding Adventure of Wheeler J. Calamity,")
London Society, Vol. 13 (1868) (three "Thumbnail Sketches" by Gilbert)
On the Cards: Routledge's Christmas Annual (1867) ("Diamonds," and "The Converted Clown,")

Other Books
The Pinafore Picture Book, 1908, retelling the story of H.M.S. Pinafore for children, in prose narrative
The Story of The Mikado, 1921, a similar retelling of The Mikado for children

Plays and Musical Stage Works
Selected stage works that were important to Gilbert's career or were otherwise notable, in chronological order, excluding those listed under other headings below:

Dulcamara, or the Little Duck and the Great Quack (1866)
La Vivandière (1867)
Harlequin Cock Robin and Jenny Wren (1867), a Christmas pantomime.
The Merry Zingara (1868)
Robert the Devil (1868), it opened the Gaiety Theatre, London and ran in the provinces for 3 years.
The Pretty Druidess (1869), a parody of Norma – the last of Gilbert's five "operatic burlesques"
An Old Score (1869) (rewritten as "Quits!" in 1872) Gilbert's first full-length comedy.
The Princess (1870). Musical farce; the precursor to Princess Ida.
The Palace of Truth (1870).
Creatures of Impulse (1871), music by Alberto Randegger. From Gilberts story "A Strange Old Lady".
Pygmalion and Galatea (1871).
Randall's Thumb (1871). A comedy that opened the Royal Court Theatre.

The Wicked World (1873).
The Happy Land (1873). This work was briefly banned for its sharp satire of government ministers.
The Realm of Joy (1873).
The Wedding March (1873) a farce adapted from Un Chapeau de Paille d'Italie.
Rosencrantz & Guildenstern (published 1874, performed 1891). Gilbert's burlesque of Hamlet.
Charity (1874). Concerns Victorian attitudes towards sex outside of marriage.
Sweethearts (1874).
Tom Cobb (1875).
Broken Hearts (1875). The last of Gilbert's "fairy comedies", this was one of Gilbert's favourite plays.
Dan'l Druce, Blacksmith (1876).
Engaged (1877).
The Ne'er-do-Weel (1878); rewritten as "The Vagabond" after a few weeks.
The Forty Thieves (1878). Co-written with three other writers, WSG played Harlequin.
Gretchen (1879)
Foggerty's Fairy (1881)
Brantinghame Hall (1888) Gilbert's biggest flop, it sent producer Rutland Barrington into bankruptcy.
The Fortune Hunter (1897). Its reception provoked WSG to announce retiring from writing for the stage.
The Fairy's Dilemma (1904).
The Hooligan (1911).

German Reed Entertainments
Gilbert wrote six one-act musical entertainments for the German Reeds between 1869 and 1875. They were successful in their own right and also helped form Gilbert's mature style as a dramatist.

No Cards (1869)
Ages Ago (1869). Gilbert's first collaboration with Frederic Clay, ran for 350 performances.
Our Island Home (1870)
A Sensation Novel (1871)
Happy Arcadia (1872)
Eyes and No Eyes (1875)

Early Comic Operas
The Gentleman in Black (1870; music by Frederic Clay). The score is lost.
Les Brigands (1871), an English adaptation of Jacques Offenbach's operetta.
Topsyturveydom (1874; music by Alfred Cellier). The score is lost.
Princess Toto (1876; music by Frederic Clay). A three-act opera.

Later Operas (Without Sullivan)
Though not as popular as the works with Arthur Sullivan, a few of Gilbert's later works arguably have stronger plots than the last two Gilbert and Sullivan operas.

The Mountebanks (1892; music; Alfred Cellier). This is the "lozenge plot" that Sullivan declined to set on several occasions.
Haste to the Wedding (1892; music; George Grossmith). An unsuccessful adaptation of The Wedding March.

His Excellency (1894; music; Osmond Carr). Gilbert felt that if Sullivan had set it, the piece would have been "another Mikado".

Fallen Fairies (1909; music by Edward German). Gilbert's last opera, which was a failure.

The Yarn of the Nancy Bell, with music by Alfred Plumpton. One of the Bab Ballads. 1869.

Thady O'Flynn, with music by James L. Molloy. 1868. From No Cards.

Would You Know that Maiden Fair, with music by Frederic Clay. From Ages Ago. c. 1869.

Corisande, with music by James L. Molloy. 1870.

Eily's Reason, with music by James L. Molloy. 1871.

Three songs from A Sensation Novel: "The Detective's Song", "The Tyrannical Bridegroom", and "The Jewel". 1871

The Distant Shore, with music by Arthur Sullivan. 1874.

The Love that Loves me Not, with music by Arthur Sullivan. 1875.

Sweethearts, with music by Arthur Sullivan. 1875.

Let Me Stay, with music by Walter Maynard. 1875.

Arthur Sullivan – His Other Works

Operas

The Sapphire Necklace (ca. 1863; unperformed)

Cox and Box (1866)

The Contrabandista (1867)

The Zoo (1875)

Ivanhoe (1891)

Haddon Hall (1892)

The Chieftain (1894)

The Beauty Stone (1898)

The Rose of Persia (1899)

The Emerald Isle (1901; completed by Edward German)

Incidental Music to Plays

The Tempest (1861)

The Merchant of Venice (1871)

The Merry Wives of Windsor (1874)

Henry VIII (1877)

Macbeth (1888)

Tennyson's The Foresters (1892)

J. Comyns Carr's King Arthur for Henry Irving (1895)

Sheet Music

Ballets and Song Cycle

L'Île Enchantée (1864 ballet)
Victoria and Merrie England (1897 ballet)
The Window; or, The Song of the Wrens (1871 song cycle)

The Masque at Kenilworth (1864)
The Prodigal Son (Sullivan) (1869)
On Shore and Sea (1871)
Festival Te Deum (1872)
The Light of the World (Sullivan) (1873)
The Martyr of Antioch (1880)
Ode for the Opening of the Colonial and Indian Exhibition (1886)
The Golden Legend (1886)
Ode for the Laying of the Foundation Stone of The Imperial Institute (1887)
Te Deum Laudamus (1902; performed posthumously)

Overture in D (1858; now lost)
Overture The Feast of Roses (1860; now lost)
Procession March (1863)
Princess of Wales's March (1863)
Symphony in E, "Irish" (1866)
Overture in C, "In Memoriam" (1866)
Concerto for Cello and Orchestra (1866)
Overture Marmion (1867)
Overture di Ballo (1870)
Imperial March (1893)
The Absent-Minded Beggar March (1899)

Absent-minded Beggar (Rudyard Kipling) 1899
Arabian Love Song (Percy Bysshe Shelley) 1866
Ay de mi, My Bird (George Eliot)1874
Bid me at least Goodbye (Sydney Grundy) 1894
Birds in the Night (Lionel H. Lewin) 1869
Bride from the North (Henry F. Chorley) 1863
Care is all Fiddle-dee-dee (F. C. Burnand) 1874
Chorister, The (Fred. E. Weatherly) 1876
Christmas Bells at Sea (C. L. Kenney) 1875
County Guy (Walter Scott) 1867
Distant Shore, The (W. S. Gilbert) 1874
Dove Song (William Brough) 1869
E tu nol sai - see You Sleep (G. Mazzucato) 1889

Edward Gray (Alfred Tennyson)(1880
Ever (Mrs Bloomfield Moore) 1887
First Departure - see The Chorister (Rev. E. Munroe) 1874
Give (Adelaide Anne Procter) 1867
Golden Days (Lionel H. Lewin)1872
Guinevere! (Lionel H. Lewin) 1872
I Heard the Nightingale (Rev. C. H. Townsend) 1863
I Wish to Tune my Quiv'ring Lyre (Anacreon; trans. Lord Byron) 1868
I Would I were a King (Victor Hugo; trans. A. Cockburn) 1878
Ich möchte hinaus es jauchzen (A. Corrodi) 1859
If Doughty Deeds (Robert Graham of Gartmore) 1866
In the Summers Long Ago (J. P. Douglas) 1867
Let Me Dream Again (B. C. Stephenson) 1875
Lied, mit Thränen halbgeschrieben (Eichendorff)1861
Life that Lives for You (Lionel H. Lewin) 1870
Little Darling Sleep Again (Cradle Song) (anon) 1874
Living Poems (H. W. Longfellow)1874
Longing for Home (Jean Ingelow) 1904
Looking Back (Louisa Gray)1870
Looking Forward (Louisa Gray) 1873
Lost Chord, The (Adelaide Anne Procter) 1877
Love that Loves Me Not, The (W. S. Gilbert) 1875
Maiden's Story, The (Emma Embury) 1867
Marquis de Mincepie, The (F. C. Burnand) 1874
Mary Morison (Robert Burns) 1874
Moon in Silent Brightness, The (Bishop Reginald Heber) 1868
Mother's Dream, The (Rev. W. Barnes) 1868
My Dear and Only Love (Marquis of Montrose) 1874
My Dearest Heart (anon) 1874
My Heart is like a Silent Lute (Benjamin Disraeli) 1904
My Love - see "There Sits a Bird in Yonder Tree
My Love Beyond the Sea - see "In the Summers Long Ago"
None but I Can Say (Lionel H. Lewin)1872
O Fair Dove, O Fond Dove (Jean Ingelow) 1868
O Israel (Hosea) 1855
O Mistress Mine (William Shakespeare) 1866
O Swallow, Swallow (Alfred Tennyson) 1900
Oh Sweet and Fair (A. F. C. K.) 1868
Oh! bella mia - see "Oh! Ma Charmante"
Oh! Ma Charmante (Victor Hugo) 1872
Old Love Letters (S. K. Cowen) 1879
Once Again (Lionel H. Lewin) 1872
Orpheus with his Lute (William Shakespeare) 1866
River, The (anon) 1875
Roads Should Blossom, The (anon) 1864
Rosalind (William Shakespeare) 1866
Sad Memories (C. J. Rowe) 1869
Sailor's Grave, The (H. F. Lyte) 1872

St. Agnes' Eve (Alfred Tennyson) 1879
Shadow, A. (Adelaide Anne Procter)1886
She is not Fair to Outward View (Hartley Coleridge) 1866
Sigh no More, Ladies (William Shakespeare) 1866
Sleep My Love, Sleep (R. Whyte Melville) 1874
Snow Lies White, The (Jean Ingelow) 1868
Sometimes (Lady Lindsay of Balcarres) 1877
Sweet Day So Cool (George Herbert) 1864
Sweet Dreamer - see "Oh! Ma Charmante"
Sweethearts (W. S. Gilbert) 1875
Tears, Idle Tears (Alfred Tennyson) 1900
Tender and True (Dinah Maria Mulock) 1874
There Sits a Bird on Yonder TreeRev. (C. H. Barham) 1873
Thou art Lost to Me (anon) 1865
Thou art Weary (Adelaide Anne Procter) 1874
Thou'rt Passing Hence (Felicia Hemans) 1875
To One in Paradise (Edgar Allan Poe) 1904
Troubadour, The (Walter Scott) 1869
Village Chimes, The (C. J. Rowe) 1870
Weary Lot is Thine, Fair Maid, A (Walter Scott) 1866
We've Ploughed our Land (anon)1875
When Thou Art Near (W. J. Stewart) 1877
White Plume, The - see "The Bride from the North"
Will He Come? (Adelaide A. Procter) 1865
Willow Song, The (William Shakespeare)1866
You Sleep (B. C. Stephenson) 1889

Hymns (Title & First Line)
Adoro Te - Saviour, again to Thy dear name we raise (Arranger)
All This Night - All this night bright angels sing
Angel Voices - Angel voices, ever singing
Audite Audientes me - I heard the voice of Jesus say
Bethlehem - While shepherd's watched their flocks (Arranger)
Bishopgarth - O King of Kings, Whose reign of old
Bolwell - Thou to whom the sick and dying
Carrow - My God, I thank Thee Who has made
Chapel Royal - O love that wilt not let me go
Christus - Show me not only Jesus dying
Clarence - Winter reigneth o'er the land
Coena Domini - Draw nigh, and take the body of the Lord
Come Unto Me - Come unto Me, ye weary (Arranger)
Constance - I've found a Friend; oh, such a Friend
Coronae - Crown Him, with many crowns
Courage, Brother - Courage, brother, do not stumble
Dominion Hymn - God bless our wide dominion
Dulce Sonans - Angel voices, ever singing
Ecclesia - The church has waited long

Ellers - Saviour, again to Thy dear name we raise (Arranger)
Evelyn - In the hour of my distress
Ever Faithful - Let us with a gladsome mind
Fatherland (St. Edmund) - I'm but a stranger here
Formosa (Falfield) - Love Divine, all love excelling
Fortunatus - Welcome, happy morning!
Golden Sheaves - To Thee, O Lord, our hearts we raise
Hanford - Jesu, my Saviour, look on me
Heber (Gennesareth) - When through the torn sail
Holy City - Sing Alleluia forth in duteous praise
Hushed was the Evening Hymn - Hushed was the evening hymn
Hymn of the Homeland - The homeland, the homeland
Lacrymae - Lord, in this Thy mercy's day
Leominster - A few more years shall roll (Arranger)
Light - Holy Spirit! Come in might! (Arranger)
Litany (1) - Jesu, life of those who die
Litany (2) - Jesu, we are far away
Long Home, The - Tender Shepherd, Thou hast still'd
Lux eoi - All is bright and cheeful round us
Lux in Tenebris - Lead, kindly Light
Lux Mundi - O Jesu, Thou art standing
Marlborough - O Strength and Stay, upholding all creation (Arranger)
Mount Zion - Rock of Ages, cleft for me
Nearer Home - For ever with the Lord (Arranger)
Noel - It came upon the midnight clear (Arranger)
Old 137th - Great King of nations, hear our prayer (Arranger)
Paradise - O Paradise!
Parting - With the sweet word of peace (Arranger)
Pilgrimage - From Egypt's bondage come
Promissio Patris - Our blest Redeemer, ere He breathed
Propior Deo - Nearer, my God, to Thee
Rest - Art thou weary, art thou languid
Resurrexit - Christ is risen!
Roseate Hues, The - The roseate hues of early dawn
Safe Home - Safe home, safe home in port
St. Ann - The Son of God goes forth to war (Arranger)
St. Francis - O Father, who hast created all
St. Gertrude - Onward, Christian soldiers
St. Kevin - Come, ye faithful, raise the strain
St. Lucian - Of Thy love some gracious token
St. Luke (St. Nathaniel) - God moves in a mysterious way
St. Mary Magdalene - Saviour, when in dust to Thee
St. Millicent - Let no tears to-day be shed
St. Patrick - He is gone - a cloud of light
St. Theresa - Brightly gleams our banner
Saints of God - The Saints of God, their conflict past.
Springtime - For all Thy love and goodness (Arranger)
Strain Upraise, The - The Strain upraise in joy and praise

Thou God of Love - Thou God of Love, beneath Thy sheltering wing
Ultor Omnipotens - God the all terrible! King who ordainest
Valete -Sweet Saviour, bless us 'ere we go
Veni, Creator - Come Holy Ghost, our souls inspire
Victoria - To mourn our dead we gather here

Part Songs

The term "Part Song" is more usually applied to one where the highest part carries the melody with the other voices supplying the accompanying harmonies.

Also included here are the soprano duet, The Sisters, and the trio Sullivan composed for the play Olivia by W. G. Wills, Morn, Happy Morn.

O Lady Dear (Madrigal) - Composed 1857, unpublished.
It was a Lover and his Lass - Words by Shakespeare. Performed at the Royal Academy of Music, 1857, unpublished.
Seaside Thoughts - Words by Bernard Bartram. Composed 1857. Published 1904.
The Last Night of the Year - Words by H. F. Chorley. Published 1863.
O Hush Thee, My Babie - Words by Walter Scott. Published 1867.
The Rainy Day - Words by H. W. Longfellow. Published 1867.
Evening - Words by Lord Houghton, after Goethe. Published 1868.
Parting Gleams - Words by Aubrey de Vere. Published 1868.
Echoes - Words by Thomas Moore. Published 1868.
The Long Day Closes - Words by H. F. Chorley. Published 1868.
Joy to the Victors - Words by Walter Scott. Published 1868
The Beleaguered - Words by H. F. Chorley. Published 1868.
It Came Upon the Midnight Clear - Words by E. H. Sears. Published 1871.
Lead, Kindly Light - Words by J. H. Newman. Published 1871.
Through Sorrows Path - Words by H. Kirke White. Published 1871.
Say, Watchman, What of the Night? - Words from Isaiah. Published 1871.
The Way is Long and Dreary - Words by Adelaide Anne Procter. Published 1871.
Morn, Happy Morn - Composed for the play, Olivia by W. G. Wills. Published 1878.
The Sisters - Words by Alfred Tennyson. Published 1881.
Wreaths for our Graves - Words by L. F. Massey. Published 1898.
Fair Daffodils - Words by Robert Herrick. Published 1904.

Church Songs
By the Waters of Babylon - Composed c. 1850. Unpublished.
Sing unto the Lord - Composed 1855. Unpublished.
Psalm 103 - Composed 1856. Unpublished.
We have heard with our ears
(i) Dedicated to Sir George Smart and performed at the Chapel Royal, January 1860.
(ii) Dedicated to Rev. Thomas Helmore. 1865.
O Love the Lord - Dedicated to John Goss. 1864.
Te Deum, Jubilate, Kyrie (in D major) 1866.

O God, Thou art Worthy - Composed for the wedding of Adrian Hope, 3 June 1867. Published in 1871.
O Taste and See - Dedicated to Rev. C. H. Haweis. 1867.
Rejoice in the Lord - Composed for the wedding of Rev. R. Brown-Borthwick, 16 April 1868.
Sing, O Heavens - Dedicated to Rev. F. C. Byng. 1869.
I Will Worship - Dedicated to Rev. F. Gore Ouseley. 1871.
Two Choruses adapted from Russian Church Music, 1874.
(i) Turn Thee Again
(ii) Mercy and Truth
I Will Mention Thy Loving-kindness - Dedicated to John Stainer. 1875.
I Will Sing of Thy Power. 1877.
Hearken Unto Me, My People. 1877.
Turn Thy Face. 1878.
Who is Like unto Thee - Dedicated to Walter Parratt. 1883.
I Will Lay Me Down in Peace - Composed 1868. Published only in 1910.

Christmas Carols & Songs

Advent
Hearken unto me, my people - An Anthem for Advent or General Use. Words from Isaiah. (1877)

Christmas Carols
All this night bright angels sing - Words by W. Austin. (1870)
I Sing the Birth - Words by Ben Jonson. (1868)
It Came Upon the Midnight Clear - Words by E. H. Sears.
Part Song for Soprano Solo and Choir (1871)
Hymn Tune "Noel" (1874)
Upon the Snow-clad Earth (1876)
While Shepherds Watched - Words by Nahum Tate (1874)
Hark! What Mean those Holy Voices? - Words by John Cawood (1883)

Songs
Christmas Bells at Sea - Words by Charles Kenney (1875)
Two songs from The Miller and His Man - A Christmas Drawing Room Entertainment. Words by F. C. Burnand (1874)
The Marquis de Mincepie
Care is all Fiddle-dee-dee
The Last Night of the Year - Part Song - Words by H. F. Chorley (1863)

Chamber Music & Solo Piano
Scherzo - Piano Solo, 1857, unpublished.
Capriccio No. 2 - Piano Solo (unfinished), 1857, unpublished.
String Quartet - Performed at Leipzig, May 1859. Published 2000
Romance in G minor - For string quartet, 1859. Published 1964.
Thoughts - Two pieces for piano solo, Published by Cramer, 1862.

An Idyll - For Cello and Piano. Composed in 1865 and Published 1899.

Allegro Risoluto - Piano solo, 1866. Published only in 1974

Berceuse - Based on the theme of Hushed was the Bacon from Cox and Box but with additional material.

Day Dreams - Six pieces for piano solo. 1867

Duo Concertante - Cello and piano. 1868

Twilight - Piano solo. 1868

www.ingramcontent.com/pod-product-compliance
Lightning Source LLC
Chambersburg PA
CBHW060135050426
42448CB00010B/2135